Women's Votes
Women's Voices

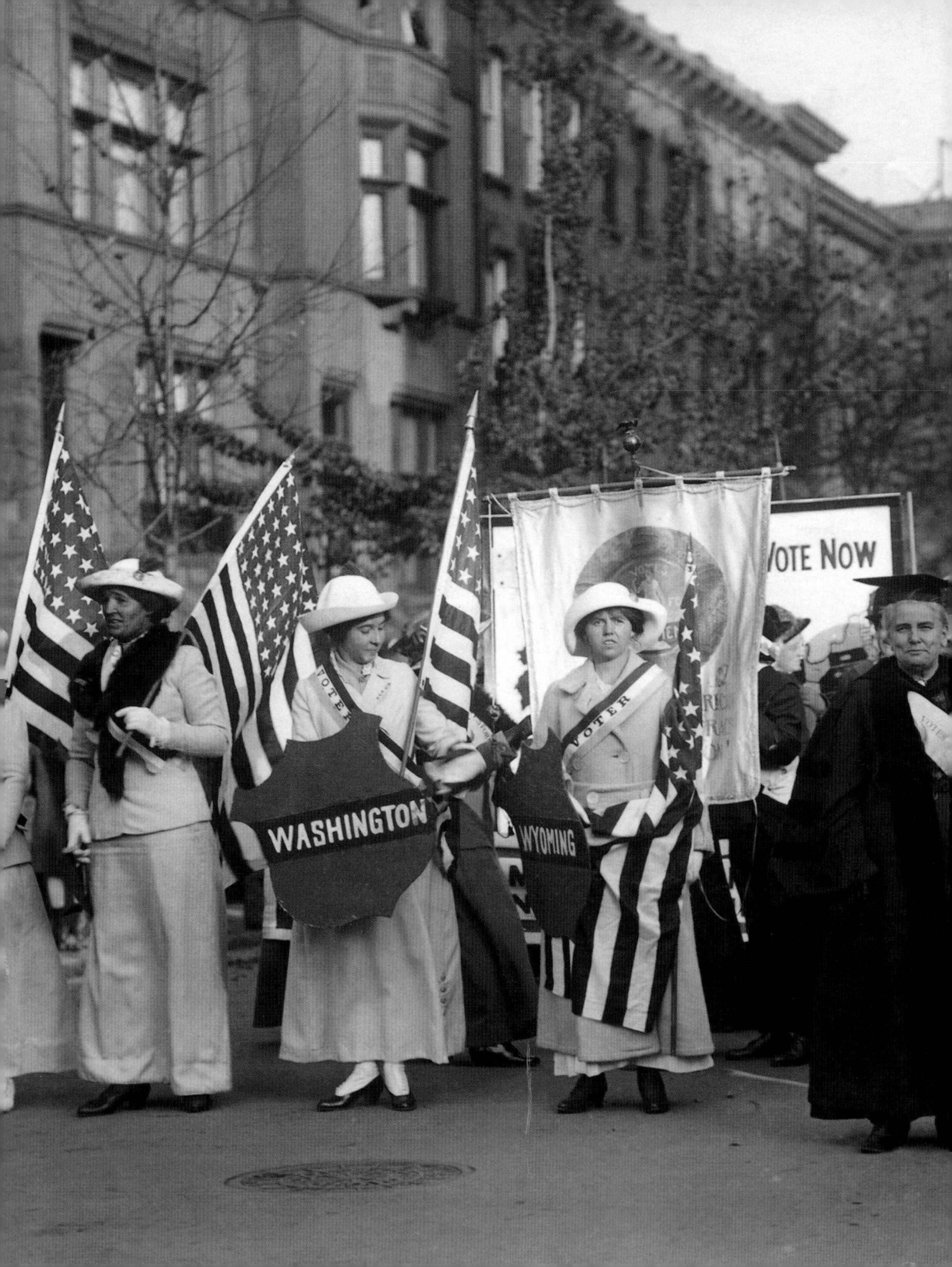
VOTE NOW
WASHINGTON
WYOMING
VOTER
VOTER

WOMEN'S VOTES WOMEN'S VOICES

The Campaign for
EQUAL RIGHTS
in **WASHINGTON**

SHANNA STEVENSON

WASHINGTON STATE HISTORICAL SOCIETY

This book was funded by the Washington Women's History Consortium. Created by State of Washington statute in 2005, the consortium is dedicated to preserving and making available resources about Washington women's history.

Printed in China by Everbest Printing Co. through Four Colour Imports, Ltd., Louisville, Kentucky.

13 12 11 10 09   4 3 2 1

Washington State Historical Society
1911 Pacific Avenue, Tacoma, Washington 98403   USA
www.WashingtonHistory.org

Library of Congress Cataloging-in-Publication Data
Stevenson, Shanna.
Women's votes, women's voices : the campaign for equal rights in Washington / Shanna Stevenson. — 1st ed.
p. cm.
Includes bibliographical references and index.
ISBN 978-0-917048-74-6 (pbk. : alk. paper)
I. Women—Suffrage—Washington (State)—History. I. Title.
JK1911.W2S74 2009
324.6'2309797—dc22
2009007456

This paper meets the minimum requirements of ANSI/NISO z39.48-1992 (Permanence of Paper).

Cover and Interior design: Kate Basart/Union Pageworks

Front cover: Suffragist Inez Milholland (right) with Mrs. O. H. P. Belmont. Harris & Ewing photo, #LC-H261-3305, Library of Congress Prints & Photographs Division, Washington, D.C.

Inside cover: Women bicyclists gather prior to a parade in support of William McKinley's presidential campaign, 1900.

Page ii: Delegates from across the nation, including Washington, participate in a 1912 pro-suffrage march in New York City.

Pages vi-vii: A gathering of Spokane's Pierian Literary Club members, c. 1923.

To Michael, Jennifer, and Edward Stevenson—

the best of my history.

We shall some day be heeded, and . . . everybody will think it was always so, just exactly as many young people think that all the privileges, all the freedom, all the enjoyments which woman now possesses always were hers. They have no idea of how every single inch of ground that she stands upon today has been gained by the hard work of some little handful of women of the past.

—SUSAN B. ANTHONY, *HISTORY OF WOMAN SUFFRAGE*

Contents

Foreword

The great thing about history is that it is always changing. True, those with a simplistic understanding of the subject are exasperated by the notion that what was once "truth" is now no longer so, but that is less a personal failing than the function of overselling what history is to begin with.

The root of the problem is a misunderstanding of the difference between the past and history. They are not the same thing. The past is what it is, or was what it was—the totality of the human experience for billions of people over tens of thousands of years. Only the barest portion of that record is visible or accessible or even understandable, sort of like gazing at the night sky and trying to comprehend the universe. There is an objective reality to it, but its immensity makes only the tiniest bits of it perceptible.

History, on the other hand, is purely a subjective enterprise, the part of it, at least, that most people are drawn to—the story. Sure, history draws on objective reality, certain "raw facts" that are indisputable by rational people, such as the certainty that women gained the right to vote in the state of Washington in November 1910. But it is the narrative arc in such constituent parts as dramatic convention, the moral of the story, and the perspective or vantage point of the storyteller that differentiates history from the past. Since the past cannot tell its own story, we are left with the human device that sees patterns in the past—history.

Such is the context, it seems to me, surrounding the emergence of women's history as a compelling subject matter. Considered from a certain biological angle, women have always been half of the story, but it was rarely a told, let alone remembered, story. In that sense, women's history is a "found story"—always there to be discerned but rarely reflected upon, at least in the conventional media of contemplation and reflection, not the least of which include classrooms and publications.

For this volume Shanna Stevenson has plied the archives and an extensive secondary literature about the women's suffrage movement to relate a chapter in the truly overarching theme of the American master narrative. I refer to the promise and sense of mission and direction that our nation's founding instrument, the Declaration of Independence, set forth as our purpose in history—namely, that all of mankind is created equal. In no small measure, the arc of our nation's history, that which has distinguished us in the broad pattern of world history, is our commitment to the ever-broadening concept of civil rights.

As Shanna shows in these pages, Washington has been, and continues to be, a bellwether jurisdiction when it comes to the salience of the women's suffrage movement and the role of women in public life. Indeed, the central episode in this book, the campaign resulting in the permanent right of women to vote in Washington, only the fifth state to do so, was the proverbial tipping point resulting in the Nineteenth Amendment to the United States Constitution, allowing women the right to vote nationally. More recently, Washington has had more expression of women as civic leaders than any other state in the Union.

Not too long ago I was at the National Archives in Washington, D.C. where I had an opportunity to view a copy of the Magna Carta and, of course, the Declaration of Independence and the Constitution. It was heartening, quite honestly, to see people line up to view these transcendent documents. My attention was riveted on a document I had not noticed on my previous visits, perhaps a function of a raised awareness derived from the suffrage centennial here in Washington. I refer to Elizabeth Cady Stanton's petition to Congress, dated January 13, 1874, and co-signed by the estimable Susan B. Anthony. Its concluding line reads: "We demand of Congress further legislation that shall forever secure to women their civil and political rights." It was, I dare say, written in a forceful hand, an observation one could only glean from looking at the original.

The rotunda of the National Archives is a considerable distance in time and space from my youth

ONE OF THE ORIGINAL "MERCER GIRLS," ELIZABETH ORDWAY (1828-1897) BECAME THE FIRST ELECTED SUPERINTENDENT OF KITSAP COUNTY PUBLIC SCHOOLS AND AN ACTIVE SUPPORTER OF THE WASHINGTON WOMEN'S SUFFRAGE MOVEMENT.

EIGHT AFRICAN AMERICAN "ROSIE THE RIVETERS" POSE IN
FRONT OF A B-29 AT BOEING'S RENTON PLANT, C. 1943.

in Seneca Falls, New York. I was born there almost exactly 100 years after the first women's suffrage convention in July 1848. One of my best friends lived across the street from the Stanton House, and another's back lot adjoined the former domicile of the famous reformer, Amelia Bloomer. The map in the visitor's guide to the Women's Rights National Historical Park shows this neighborhood—the one where I grew up.

Such are the kinds of meanings, memories, even reveries, that forthright historical storytelling can bring forth, especially one as redemptive as the struggle for civil rights. I'm confident you will find purpose and meaning, as well, in the reading of *Women's Votes, Women's Voices.*

—DAVID L. NICANDRI

October 30, 2008

Marked by political intrigue, controversy, hard work, and even some frivolity, the fight for women's right to vote in the state of Washington is an inspiring story of women speaking out and organizing for change. In a struggle that lasted more than a half century, women campaigned for and twice won the right to vote in Washington during both the territorial and state periods. Women first achieved the vote in the 1880s, only to lose it through court decisions. Still, women continued to fight for civic equality by forming coalitions—notably with farmers and labor organizations—after statehood was achieved in 1889 and into the early twentieth century. Finally, through a strategically organized,

grassroots campaign fueled by Progressive Era sensibilities, women persuaded Washington men to vote in 1910 for an amendment to the state constitution enacting permanent voting rights for women. It was only a partial victory, however, because most Native American women, some Asian women, and women who could not read and speak English continued to be denied the vote.

As the fifth state nationally—and the first in the twentieth century—to permanently enact women's voting rights, Washington's 1910 victory was a pivotal event in a revitalized national suffrage movement. Along with their counterparts in other primarily western states, Washington women played an important role in advocating for what would become the Nineteenth Amendment to the United States Constitution in 1920, ensuring women's right to vote nationally. Their 1910 victory empowered Washington women to vote in all elections, including presidential and congressional contests. They not only gained a voice in self-government but also made their mark in the great human struggle for equal rights.

After 1910 women used the vote to support laws, policies, and governmental actions reflecting the concerns of women, children, and families. Washington women also supported World War I home-front efforts in common with men and joined other activist campaigns. During the 1930s and 1940s many women served in capacities outside their homes—in relief efforts, factory work, and military service. Hearkening back to the so-called first wave of feminists of the nineteenth century, second-wave feminists in the 1960s and 1970s re-energized Washington women and the fight for equal rights—a struggle that continues today.

—SHANNA STEVENSON

Acknowledgments

I wish to acknowledge Heather Lee Miller, David Nicandri, Garry Schalliol, Michael Stevenson, and Christina Dubois for their editing work. For their help in reviewing and commenting, thanks to Karen Blair, Susan Armitage, Doris Pieroth and Sue Lean. Kevin Hanken provided important support and inspiration came from Kim Jensen, Jennifer Ross-Nazzal, Tom Edwards, and my own favorite Washington suffragists, Mary Olney Brown and Dr. Cora Smith Eaton King.

ALICE PAUL UNFURLING THE RATIFICATION BANNER FROM THE BALCONY OF
THE NATIONAL WOMAN'S PARTY HEADQUARTERS IN LAFAYETTE SQUARE,
WASHINGTON, D.C.

Abbreviations

AWSA	American Woman Suffrage Association
AYPE	Alaska-Pacific-Yukon Exposition
CU	Congressional Union
EFS	Equal Franchise Society
ESL	Equal Suffrage League
HWS	History of Woman Suffrage
NAWSA	National American Woman Suffrage Association
NCWV	National Council of Women Voters
NLWS	National League for Woman's Service
NWP	National Woman's Party
NWSA	National Woman Suffrage Association
WCOM-PTA	Washington Congress of Mothers and Parent-Teacher Associations
WCTU	Woman's Christian Temperance Union
WESA	Washington Equal Suffrage Association
WPEL	Washington Political Equality League
WTWSA	Washington Territory Woman's Suffrage Association

Women's Votes
Women's Voices

Gearing Up

r the Fight

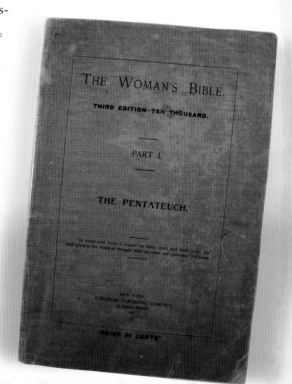

The right to vote through a free and secret ballot is one of the pillars of American democracy. In a representative form of government, voting is a fundamental aspect of public self-determination. Voting is the means by which the majority expresses its will, creating the basis of governmental authority and the rule of law. The term *suffrage* comes from the Latin word *suffragium*, which means to vote for or to support.[1] The call for women's suffrage dates to the beginning of the republic when Abigail Adams implored her husband to "remember the ladies," and others highlighted the importance of women as necessary participants in a democracy.[2] These early feminists based their case for women's right to vote on the virtues and abilities that they believed to be innate and uniquely feminine. As early as the mid 1700s women voted sporadically in the American

ELIZABETH CADY STANTON (1815–1902) WAS A PRIMARY
ORGANIZER OF THE FIRST WOMEN'S RIGHTS CONVENTION
AND A COAUTHOR OF THE DECLARATION OF SENTIMENTS
IN 1848. *THE WOMAN'S BIBLE*, ORIGINALLY PUBLISHED
IN 1895, WAS PERHAPS HER MOST CONTROVERSIAL
PROPOSAL. THROUGH THIS BOOK STANTON AND A
COMMITTEE ATTEMPTED TO COUNTER WHAT THEY SAW AS
BIBLICAL INTERPRETATION BIASED AGAINST WOMEN.

colonies. Women voted for several years in New Jersey until 1807 when the legislature outlawed it. Succeeding generations of suffragists often allied with other reformists advocating for temperance and the abolition of slavery. ★ For the first time women categorically demanded the right to vote at the first women's rights convention in 1848. Elizabeth Cady Stanton, a well-educated, reform-minded young mother, with Lucretia Coffin Mott, a Quaker, her sister Martha Coffin Wright, and two Quaker women from Waterloo, New York, organized the convention, which was held July 19 and 20, 1848, at the Wesleyan Methodist Church in Seneca Falls, New York.[3] They modeled their gathering on abolitionist meetings they had attended, from which they derived the phrase "declaration of sentiments."[4] Their declaration itself borrowed from the language and format of the Declaration of Independence. In their carefully crafted rhetoric, the authors of the Declaration of Sentiments drew pointed connections between resistance to royal oppression of the American colonists in 1776—which sparked a revolution—and resistance to men's continued oppression of women in the United States in 1848.[5] ★ Over three hundred men and women attended the convention, which accepted the Declaration of Sentiments and then adopted a series of resolutions as remedies for the unequal treatment of women. Suffrage was arguably the most controversial of the declaration's wide variety of indictments and demands. The document declared that man "has never permitted her to exercise her inalienable right to the elective franchise." The convention affirmed the resolution: "That it is the duty of women of this country to secure to themselves their sacred right to the elective franchise."[6] ★ Until after the Civil War, states and territories defined voting credentials, which often included limitations by age, race, sex, property ownership, criminality, mental ability, literacy, religion, and the ability to pay poll taxes. Often referred to

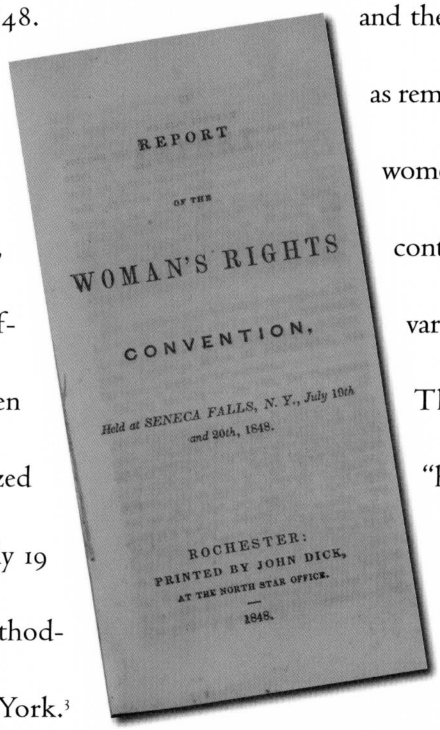

REPORT

OF THE

WOMAN'S RIGHTS

CONVENTION,

Held at SENECA FALLS, N. Y., July 19th and 20th, 1848.

ROCHESTER:
PRINTED BY JOHN DICK,
AT THE NORTH STAR OFFICE.
—
1848.

as a *franchise*, the term *voting* signifies not a right but a privilege. During Reconstruction, the ratification of the Fourteenth and Fifteenth amendments to the United States Constitution in 1868 and 1870 changed the qualifications for voting. The Fourteenth Amendment inserted the word "male" into the Constitution for the first time when the second section of the amendment defined the basis of congressional representation to include "male persons over the age of twenty-one."[7] The Fifteenth Amendment stated that the right to vote could not be "denied or abridged . . . on account of race, color, or previous condition of servitude," but sex was not listed as one of the "prohibited disenfranchisements."[8] ★ Support for these amendments caused a serious rift among suffragists and abolitionists. These two groups had worked together for voting reform and equality before and during the Civil War under the aegis of the American Equal Rights Association (AERA). Some reformers advocated black men's right to vote ahead of women's. This faction—headed by Lucy Stone and Henry Blackwell, among others— believed that forcing the issue of women's suffrage alongside that of black men might prevent newly freed African American men from winning the vote; as a result, they formed the American Woman Suffrage Association (AWSA) in 1869. Other ardent suffragists, like Elizabeth Cady Stanton and Susan B. Anthony, were enraged by the idea that black men would be able to vote before white women. This latter group formed the National Woman Suffrage Association (NWSA) in 1869, and the movement to advocate women's suffrage became separate from other reforms. ★ The western territories of Wyoming (1869) and Utah (1870) were the first post-Civil War jurisdictions in which women achieved full enfranchisement, followed by Washington Territory in 1883. However, the Washington Territorial Supreme Court revoked women's right to vote in 1888, as Congress had done in Utah Territory in 1887 as part of an act outlawing polygamy. Full women's suffrage in the states of Wyoming, Colorado, Utah, and Idaho preceded the success in Washington in 1910. Ten other states enacted full women's suffrage before 1920 when the Nineteenth Amendment to the Constitution enfranchised women nationally.[9]

Suffrage in Washington Territory

*W*omen already played locally significant social, economic, and political roles prior to enfranchisement in Washington. Before Euro-American exploration and settlement in the Northwest, Native American women often held leadership positions in their tribal groups. They were the keepers of oral traditions and managed vital food gathering and processing functions. Some Indian women married Hudson's Bay Company employees and, later, other non-Indians who moved to the area from the mid nineteenth century on, a practice that helped bridge the gulf between Native American and Euro-American culture.[10] Native American women today represent a significant number of tribal government officials in the region, continuing their long tradition of leadership.

By the mid 1840s emigrants were moving in growing numbers to what was then called the Oregon Country (encompassing what is now Washington as well as parts of Idaho, Montana, and Wyoming). By endowing women with important property rights, the federal Oregon Donation Act of 1850 provided an incentive for families and women to settle the Northwest. The law reflected a growing trend among states and territories to give married women rights over property.[11] For example, under this law, a married couple settling in the territory before 1850 could claim up to 640 free acres of land, with half in the wife's name. For settlers coming to the area after 1850, the amount of acreage available was halved, but the joint-ownership provision remained the same. Spurred by population growth as settlers took advantage of the Oregon Donation Act, Washington separated from Oregon Territory in 1853. For women, the attainment of property rights and partnership status with their husbands was an important step toward equal rights in what eventually became the state of Washington.[12]

Unencumbered by the layers of legal and social restrictions placed on women by legislation and custom in the East, mid-nineteenth-century lawmakers in new western territories like Washington often incorporated reformist views of women's rights into law. The federal organic act creating Washington Territory in 1853 empowered the territorial assembly to determine voter qualifications. In 1854, just six years after the Declaration of Sentiments was signed at Seneca Falls, Seattle legislator Arthur A. Denny proposed women's suffrage in the first meeting of the Washington Territorial Legislature in Olympia. Denny proposed to amend a pending bill relating to voting "to allow all white females over the age of 18 years to vote," but it failed in the house of representatives by a vote of 8–9.[13]

Despite Denny's noble efforts, Washington's first voting law ultimately gave the franchise to "all white male inhabitants of twenty-one years, of three months' residence, provided they were citizens of the United States, or had declared their intentions to become such." The legislature added a proviso allowing mixed-blood Indian men "who have adopted the customs and habits of civilization" to vote.[14]

Although they could not vote on most territorial matters, Washington Territory women apparently had a voice in granting liquor licenses. The territorial legislature on January 28, 1857, passed a law requiring approval by "a majority of all the adult white inhabitants of the election precinct wherein such grocer is to be located."[15] The legislature again altered voter qualifications in 1866, restricting the voting rights of Confederate Civil War veterans and imposing land ownership and literacy requirements on mixed-blood (Native American) voters. The 1867 territorial voting law also clearly stated that "all white American citizens twenty-one years of age" had the right to vote.[16]

ARTHUR A. DENNY (1822–1899) OF SEATTLE WAS THE FIRST TERRITORIAL LAWMAKER TO INTRODUCE LEGISLATION THAT WOULD HAVE GIVEN WASHINGTON WOMEN THE RIGHT TO VOTE.

Catharine Paine Blaine

The first women's rights convention in the nation—at Seneca Falls, New York, in 1848—was set against the backdrop of change and reform brought about by the Second Great Awakening, which created political, economic, and social upheaval in the United States. Worldwide, the year 1848 was marked by struggles for political change in many parts of the world including France, Germany, and England. The reforms expressed in the Declaration of Sentiments forged at Seneca Falls—the first comprehensive list of women's rights in the United States—were incorporated in the new territorial governments of the West that were just forming during the mid nineteenth century. Catharine Paine Blaine, one of the signers of the Declaration of Sentiments, and others who came from the East brought these reform ideas to Washington Territory. ☆ Catharine Paine, a resident of Seneca Falls and a devout member of the Methodist Episcopal Church, was just eighteen when she added her signature to the Declaration of Sentiments as one of the 68 women and 32 men signers on July 20, 1848. Little is known about Paine's activities in Seneca Falls or why she signed the Declaration of Sentiments. Her participation may have been related to her religious affiliations and her firm belief in abolition and, by extension, the rights of women as citizens. ☆ In 1853 Catharine Paine married David Blaine in Seneca Falls after a courtship formed through their shared religious beliefs. The same year, the Methodist Episcopal Church called Blaine to the Oregon Territory, where he was instructed to report to Puget Sound. Catharine and David Blaine took a honeymoon voyage from New York across the Isthmus of Panama, reaching Seattle and their new pastorate in November 1853. Upon arriving in Seattle the couple stayed briefly with the Arthur and Mary Ann Boren Denny family, also Methodists. Denny had been elected to the first territorial house of representatives after the creation of Washington Territory in 1853. It may only be a coincidence that Denny introduced the women's suffrage legislation in 1854, shortly after the Blaines' visit, but his action created an important connection between the Seneca Falls Convention and the start of Washington's suffrage movement. ☆ Catharine Blaine established the first subscription school in Seattle in January 1854 and taught Sabbath School for her husband's church. After founding the church there, the Blaines left Seattle in 1856. They went on to Oregon and then returned to the East Coast, but returned to Seattle in 1882. Catharine Blaine was on the voter registration rolls in 1885 when women voted in Washington. She died in 1908, two years before Washington women achieved their permanent suffrage victory.[17]

REV. DAVID E. BLAINE AND FAMILY IN 1856.

Catharine Paine Blaine (1829-1908) was one of the signers of the Declaration of Sentiments in 1848 in Seneca Falls, New York. She married David Blaine, moved to Seattle in 1853, and had a son in 1856.

Women First Vote in Washington Territory

*T*his territorial law empowering "all white American citizens" to vote became the rallying point for Washington suffragists who also cited the 1868 Fourteenth Amendment to the Constitution as defining citizens as "all persons born or naturalized in the United States." Together, they said, these laws enabled women to vote outright. Bellingham legislator and suffragist Edward Eldridge was one of those who urged women as citizens to exercise this right.[18] In 1869 suffragist Mary Olney Brown determined to test the 1867 law. When she announced her intention to vote, many in her hometown of White River tried to dissuade her. She went to the polls anyway, accompanied by her husband, daughter, and son-in-law. When opposed, Brown argued that she was a citizen and, as such, should be accorded the right to vote under the Fourteenth Amendment to the Constitution. Brown and her daughter proffered their ballots, but election judges refused to accept them out of fear that they would sully the precinct's returns.[19]

Undaunted, Brown launched her own suffrage campaign the following year, writing several newspaper editorials urging women to vote.[20] By 1870 she had moved to Olympia, and her sister Charlotte Emily Olney French was living in Grand Mound, in southern Thurston County. With other women in the area, the sisters planned a picnic dinner near Grand Mound at the schoolhouse at Goodell's Point, where the June 6, 1870, election was to be held. French, like her sister, was well-versed in the arguments for women's suffrage and spoke at the gathering. After the picnic, the women—seven in all—handed in their ballots. The husband of one of the women was an election inspector for that precinct; this may have had something to do with their ballots being accepted. Women of nearby Black River (present-day Littlerock) had stationed a man on a "fleet horse" at the Grand Mound precinct to report whether the women there had been allowed to vote. The man arrived at the polling place waving his hat and yelling, "They're voting! They're voting!" Eight Black River women immediately cast their ballots.

While the southern Thurston County women were successful, a small Olympia delegation was not. When Brown and two women presented ballots at the Olympia courthouse, they were rejected despite Brown's legal arguments and threats of prosecution against the election officials.[21] The local *Olympia Transcript* verified that the fifteen votes cast by women from Grand Mound and Black River (also known as Miami) precincts had been included in the election results.[22] Although those fifteen votes did not constitute a permanent stride toward suffrage in Washington, they provided a significant stepping-stone in the overall history of the movement.

Feminists around the country attempting to vote during this period argued that women were entitled to do so under the Fourteenth Amendment (1868). Proponents of this strategy, often referred to as the New Departure movement, considered voting to be one of the "privileges and immunities of citizenship" mentioned in the amendment. Furthermore, the Fifteenth Amendment (1870) guaranteed suffrage as a basic right of citizenship.[23] Reconstruction feminists determined, according to historian Ellen Carol Dubois, to pursue a broad interpretation of the amendments to include women's rights along with those of freedmen.[24] In 1872 noted eastern suffragist Susan B. Anthony attempted to vote in Rochester, New York, but was arrested and later convicted of casting an illegal vote.[25] The United States Supreme Court finally dismissed the legality of "New Departure" voting in the 1870s with its decision in a suit brought by Missouri suffragist Virginia Minor, which determined that the right to vote was not an automatic right of citizenship.[26] After this defeat, suffragists switched tactics and pursued a separate constitutional amendment instead of advocating that women's right to vote was inherent in the broad interpretation of democracy as defined in the Constitution.[27]

Susan B. Anthony Inspires Washington

*I*n autumn 1871 women's rights leaders Susan B. Anthony and Abigail Scott Duniway toured the Northwest, accelerating the women's suffrage movement in Washington Territory. Duniway was already a well-known suffragist in Oregon. She had started the first women's rights newspaper in the region, *The New Northwest*, in May 1871. Accompanied by her husband Benjamin, Duniway traveled with Anthony as her tour manager, taking lessons on how to run a suffrage campaign.

Their sojourn was not without controversy. Traveling to Walla Walla in September, Anthony and Duniway were dogged by a flap over Anthony's earlier visit with a Umatilla, Oregon, bartender whose mother had known her in Rochester. When they arrived in Walla Walla, churches refused to host Anthony, stating that she had sipped an alcoholic beverage during the Umatilla meeting.[28] After her departure a local newspaper summed up the campaign for women's right to vote by stating that it was "worse than the small-pox and chills and fever combined."[29]

The women regrouped in Portland, then endured a difficult stage trip from Monticello on the Cowlitz River (near present-day Longview) to Olympia, the territorial capital, where Anthony spoke on October 17 to an audience of about one hundred, including some legislators. Attendees paid a one-dollar admission fee, which Anthony donated to benefit victims of the recent Chicago fire. John Miller Murphy, *Washington Standard* editor and an avowed suffragist, described her arguments as "graceful and elegant."[30]

Two days later Anthony and Duniway addressed the legislature by means of an invitation initiated by Representative Daniel Bigelow through a joint resolution. Bigelow and his wife Ann Elizabeth White were active in the early women's suffrage movement. A native New Yorker, Bigelow had honed his views on women's rights as a law student at Harvard in the 1840s before coming to Olympia in 1851 where he became an important figure in

FACING PAGE, LEFT: MARY OLNEY BROWN (1821–1886) GAVE BIRTH TO ELEVEN CHILDREN, AND WAS A MIDWIFE AND POET WHO WROTE ELOQUENTLY ABOUT WOMEN'S SUFFRAGE.

FACING PAGE, RIGHT: EMILY OLNEY FRENCH (1828–1897) JOINED HER SISTER IN THE FIGHT FOR WASHINGTON WOMEN'S SUFFRAGE AND WAS ONE OF THE FEW SUCCESSFUL FEMALE VOTERS IN THURSTON COUNTY IN 1870.

THIS PAGE: SUSAN B. ANTHONY (1820–1906) CAME TO WASHINGTON IN 1871 TO TOUR THE TERRITORY, INSPIRE SUFFRAGISTS, AND HELP CREATE THE FIRST TERRITORY-WIDE SUFFRAGE ORGANIZATION.

early territorial politics. The day before her legislative speech, Anthony dined at the Bigelows' Olympia home, now the Bigelow House Museum. Bigelow had introduced a women's suffrage bill on October 14, but Bigelow and Anthony differed in their approach to winning women's suffrage. Bigelow thought that women should vote on whether they wanted suffrage while Anthony wanted it granted outright through a declaratory act.

On October 19 legislators, including Bigelow, escorted Anthony into the chambers where a number of Olympia women viewed the proceedings. Turned out in a gray silk gown, she lauded the group, saying, "This was the first time in the history of our nation that a woman has been allowed the privilege of addressing the lawmakers in session."[31] The *Olympia Transcript* said of her speech: "Miss Anthony is a woman of more than ordinary ability, and the able manner in which she handled her subject before the Legislature, was ample warning to the members of that body who oppose woman suffrage to be silent."[32] Duniway also spoke to the legislature. The house of representatives turned down a proposal to print Anthony's legislative address, but the *Washington Standard* published a summary of it.[33]

The day after Anthony's visit to the legislature, a "declaratory" suffrage bill in line with her strat-egy was introduced, but it failed 11–13, with Bigelow voting no. Bigelow's bill authorizing women to vote on whether they wanted suffrage was postponed indefinitely on a vote of 16–11. Anthony, for her part, stated that women should not be voting on whether they wished to have suffrage, reasoning that they were being held in a condition of servitude and did not know the value of the vote. Reputedly, she was relying on Washington men to follow the lead of Wyoming, which had enacted women's suffrage in 1869 to lure women to the territory. Clearly, the Washington legislature did not buy her argument.

Anthony spoke at Tumwater and again in Olympia before embarking on a trip to Victoria, British Columbia, where she enjoyed mixed results advocating for women's votes in a community much less attuned to suffrage than Olympia.[34] Anthony and Duniway then journeyed to Whidbey Island and Port Townsend where newspapers were less than positive. The editor of the Port Townsend *Cyclop* mostly concentrated on Anthony as an "old maid" who had never kissed a man over two years old, but he also harped on the unattractive appearance of Port Townsend women generally.[35]

On October 31 Seattle suffragist Sarah Yesler hosted a dinner for Anthony, but others were not as cordial. Beria Brown, editor of the *Territorial Dispatch* proclaimed Anthony a revolutionist—"aiming at nothing less than the breaking up of the very foundations of society"—and predicted the overthrow of religious sanctity, the family circle, and children's legitimacy if women should receive the vote. He equated her stance with free love and joined Anthony's name with notorious free-love advocate Victoria Woodhull.[36]

After her swing around Puget Sound, Anthony returned to Olympia to

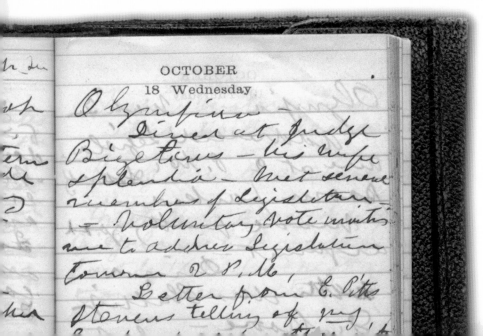

ABOVE: DANIEL RICHARDSON BIGELOW (1825–1905) AND HIS WIFE ANN ELIZABETH WHITE BIGELOW (1836–1926) WERE PROMINENT OLYMPIA SUFFRAGE ADVOCATES. THEY HOSTED SUSAN B. ANTHONY AT THEIR HOME IN 1871.

LEFT: IN HER DIARY ANTHONY CHARACTERIZES ANN BIGELOW AS "SPLENDID."

participate in Washington's first women's suffrage convention, which began on November 8, 1871. A committee including Yesler, Bigelow, and Anthony drafted the constitution for the Washington Territory Woman Suffrage Association (WTWSA), the principle outcome of the convention. Delegates also passed a series of resolutions including one asking the legislature to direct the territory's election judges to accept the ballots of women citizens in accordance with the Fourteenth Amendment.[37] At Anthony's suggestion, the group of two to three hundred men and women elected only female officers.[38] Pro-suffragists and anti-suffragists debated at the convention.[39] The association ultimately chose Anthony as its delegate to the National Woman Suffrage Association's convention, presumably to be held in New York in May 1872, and paid her $100 for expenses.

The WTWSA spurred the creation of local suffrage organizations in Olympia and Thurston County. These women likely were part of a lobby for the remainder of the 1871 legislative session, attending each day's proceedings. Legislators responded by passing a unique anti-suffrage law, which declared that women could not vote until Congress made it the law of the land. Historian G. Thomas Edwards surmised in *Sowing Good Seeds* that this unusual act might have been in response to the 1866 bill [and the 1867 bill with many of the same provisions], which had given women encouragement to vote; and that it was meant to discourage further lobbying by women, which some said wasted time. Edwards noted that Washington was likely the only territory to turn the issue of women's suffrage over to the federal government.[40]

Abigail Scott Duniway

Born in Illinois, Abigail Scott's family came west over the Oregon Trail to Lafayette, Oregon, in the early 1850s. Her mother and brother died on the crossing. After a brief teaching career she married Benjamin Duniway in 1853, and the couple eventually had six children. After her husband was injured, Abigail became the family's breadwinner, first opening a millinery shop and then, in 1871, starting publication of her own women's rights newspaper, *The New Northwest.* ☆ Duniway traveled to Washington with Susan B. Anthony in 1871. She campaigned ardently for women's suffrage in Idaho, Oregon, and Washington; lobbied the 1878 Constitutional Convention in Walla Walla; and was a pivotal advocate in Washington's 1883 women's suffrage victory. Although sometimes controversial in her approach to the women's rights campaign and at odds with national organizers, she was an unwavering voice on behalf of women. ☆ After Oregon enacted women's suffrage in 1912, Duniway was the first woman voter to register. She cast her first ballot in 1914 and died one year later.[41]

After more than four decades of advocating for women's suffrage, a happy and proud Abigail Scott Duniway (1834–1915) cast her first ballot in Oregon in 1914.

Community Property Laws

Despite many failures, in 1869 the legislature strengthened the legal status of women with the enactment of Washington's first community property law, modeled on California's code, which itself reflected Spanish civil law. The statute specified that property acquired after marriage by either husband or wife or both became community property, legally owned by both parties. Husbands continued to retain many rights over community assets but could not dispose of them without the wife's consent. The law was modified in 1873, 1879, and 1881. The legislation contributed to the evolving status of married women's property laws in the United States, in which governments recognized women's changing familial roles, their increased education, and public service. Although "almost every state and territory adopted a married women's property act between 1835 and 1850," according to law professor Richard H. Chused, the exact reasons for enactment of Washington's version in 1869, twenty years before statehood, remain unclear.[42] One idea is that the law brought the territory into alignment with California, a dominant force in West Coast law. Others believe the goal was to attract more women to Washington.[43]

In 1972 the Washington State Legislature substantially revised the community property law so that both husband and wife had equal power to manage community property; this statute remains in force today.[44] Even in 2008 only nine other states besides Washington—Alaska (opt-in), Arizona, California, Idaho, Louisiana, Nevada, New Mexico, Texas, and Wisconsin—had community property laws.[45]

Women Vote in School Elections

Because schools were associated with their traditional sphere of home and family, women voted in school elections as early as 1838 in Kentucky. Likewise, in Washington Territory, women could vote in school elections well before they achieved full suffrage. Statutory language about this right to vote in school elections was unclear. In 1854 the Washington legislature defined eligible school electors as "every inhabitant of twenty-one years, who was a resident in the district three months and who was a taxpayer."[46] In 1855 the legislature changed the law to read "white American citizens and other white male inhabitants of twenty-one years and none other." In 1858 the legislature qualified voting rights in school elections as it had in 1854, but restricted it to "males" in 1860 and to "white males" in 1863.[47] Whether any women voted in school elections under these provisions is undocumented. By 1871 the legislature had adopted clearer language for qualifying women to vote in school district elections, describing the electorate as every tax-paying district inhabitant over age twenty-one.[48] In 1877 the territorial legislature authorized women to vote in school board director elections in their local districts, but they could not vote for county superintendents.[49]

Ongoing Territorial Suffrage Efforts

Throughout the 1870s the WTWSA continued its work and the territorial legislature considered various suffrage measures. In 1873 Edward Eldridge introduced a women's suffrage bill, which lost 12–18 in the house of representatives. In 1875 Olympia legislator Elwood Evans, then speaker of the house, introduced another suffrage bill, which was again defeated—this time 11–15. An effort to repeal the definitive law of 1871 that precluded women's suffrage until Congress took action also failed.[50]

Eldridge used an expediency argument in advocating for suffrage, stating, "I consider there is nothing that would so promote the welfare and prosperity of our nation and the happiness of the

whole human race as the disenthrallment and elevation of women."[51] Women used both expediency and justice arguments in Washington and nationally. The former posited that women should have the vote in order to accomplish specific ends, such as moral reforms or attracting women to certain geographic areas. Adherents of the justice argument contended that women inherently deserved the right to vote without having to detail what the franchise would accomplish. Pragmatic suffragists changed tactics in order to appeal to specific constituencies as circumstances dictated. According to suffrage historian Rebecca Mead, part of the winning strategy in the West involved employing rationales for suffrage that varied to fit the political climate.[52]

The Walla Walla Convention

Frustrated by the vassalage of being a territory, the 1877 Washington legislature authorized a state constitutional convention in Walla Walla for the following year. Upon learning of the proclamation, Olympia suffragist Mary Olney Brown determined to make every effort to secure pro-suffrage delegates and petition them to leave the word *male* out of the constitution when defining the characteristics of eligible voters. Although she tried to persuade the WTWSA to lobby for women's suffrage, they did not take any concerted action. As president of the WTWSA, Brown thus took it upon herself to send petitions throughout the territory and write articles for publication in regional publications like *The New Northwest* and *Olympia Courier*.[53] Convention delegates received petitions signed by 600 men and women urging inclusion of women's suffrage in the new state constitution.[54]

Duniway spoke at the convention, requesting that the word *male* be omitted from the constitutional requirements for voting. Eldridge, a delegate and steadfast suffrage supporter, backed her. Several Walla Walla suffragists worked at buttonholing delegates.[55] The convention drafted two separate articles related to women's suffrage—one for women's right to vote and one for women's right to vote and hold office. Despite passage of the constitution by a vote of 6,462–3,231, both suffrage articles failed.[56] Congress, however, did not act on what turned out to be a premature statehood initiative for Washington, so the issue was moot.[57]

In 1881 the issue of women's suffrage was again before the legislature, brought to the forefront with a petition signed by fifty women.[58] Representative George Comegys, speaker of the house from Whitman County, worked with Brown to write the bill. Duniway and prominent Seattle attorney William H. White spoke at length before the legislature in its support.[59] Although the bill carried the House 13–11, it lost in council 5–7.[60] (Once Washington achieved statehood in 1889, the council became the state senate.) According to Brown, the so-called saloon lobby (brewers, saloon owners, and other anti-prohibitionists) thwarted the council effort for suffrage legislation. She noted that "as many of them as could be bought by drinks pledged themselves to vote against the bill. The members of the Council were present, and though an urgent invitation was given all to speak, not one of them denied the charge made by Mr. White [about the opposition of liquor interests]."[61]

UW27634z

Changes in the Legal Status of Women

The property ownership rights established for women under the Oregon Donation Act of 1850 and enhanced by Washington's community property laws foreshadowed the enactment of women's suffrage in territorial Washington. In 1881 Washington's legislature empowered married women to acquire, hold, enjoy, and dispose of property; sign contracts; and sue and be sued, the same as if they were unmarried. Under the legislation, parents gained equal control of children. The law changed the status of husband and wife to designate each as a half householder, and only together were married couples considered legally a "keeper of the house."[62] Previously, a woman's legal identity was subsumed in that of her husband. This legislation separated a married woman's rights from those of her husband, created legal co-sovereignty, and abolished many of the legal differences between husband and wife.[63] Nonetheless, the legislation expressly forbade women to vote.

After the enactment of these laws, both Brown and Duniway predicted victory for women's suffrage in 1883.[64] The gains from this legislation resulted in a separate legal status for married women that also qualified them for jury duty, and this jury service became the basis for court challenges to women's right to vote during the territorial period.

FACING PAGE: FIRST PAGE OF A SUFFRAGE MEMORIAL PRESENTED IN PERSON BY ABIGAIL SCOTT DUNIWAY TO THE 1878 CONSTITUTIONAL CONVENTION AT WALLA WALLA.

THIS PAGE: A WASHINGTON HOMESTEAD. THE RIGHT TO OWN PROPERTY, GRANTED TO WOMEN UNDER THE OREGON DONATION ACT, WAS AN IMPORTANT RUNG ON THE WOMEN'S RIGHTS LADDER.

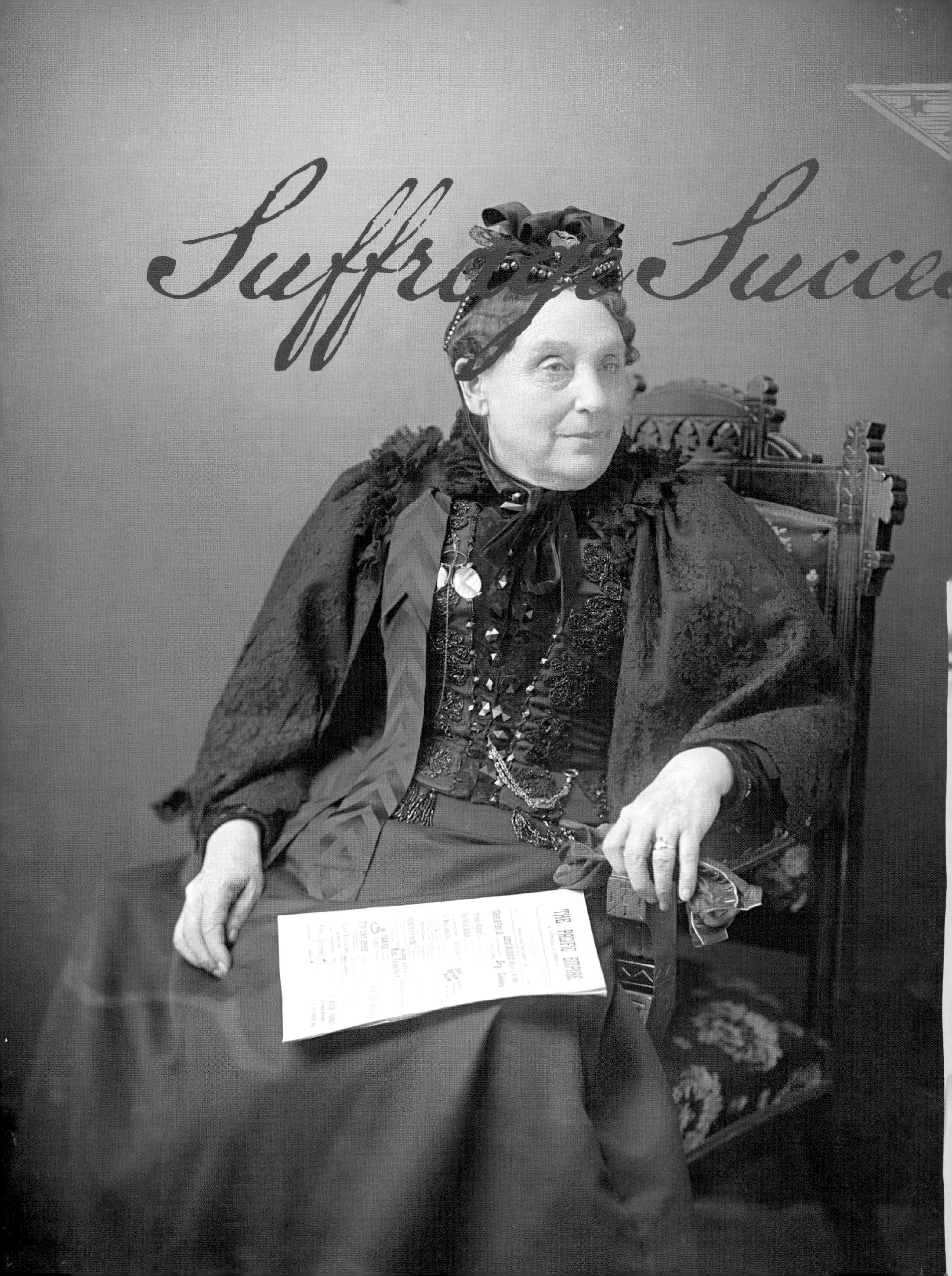
Suffrage Succe
THE PACIFIC EMPIRE

Part 2

...es and Failures

FREE SPEECH, FREE PRESS, FREE PEOPLE.

PORTLAND, OREGON, THURSDAY, SEPTEMBER 25, 1884.   PER YEAR—$3 00.

Building on gains for women during the previous decade, the suffrage movement gathered momentum in Washington after 1881. Duniway played a strong role in this movement, although opinions differed about her effectiveness as a lobbyist.[65] Some wanted to limit her efforts, but Duniway doggedly monitored the progress of the 1883 suffrage bill, often taking Olympia women with her to the legislature. "I remained at headquarters," she said, "enduring alike the open attacks of the venal press and the more covert opposition of the saloons and brothels, and, as vigilantly as I could watched all legislative movement, taking much pains to keep the public mind excited

FACING PAGE: AN OREGON TRAIL IMMIGRANT FROM ILLINOIS, ABIGAIL SCOTT DUNIWAY (1834-1915) BECAME A PILLAR OF THE WOMEN'S SUFFRAGE MOVEMENT IN THE PACIFIC NORTHWEST.

THIS PAGE: DUNIWAY PUBLISHED *THE NEW NORTHWEST* WEEKLY FROM 1871 TO 1887 IN PORTLAND. SHE INCLUDED NEWS AND SOME OF HER FICTION WRITING IN SERIALIZED FORM, AND FEATURED NEWS OF THE 1883 WASHINGTON SUFFRAGE CAMPAIGN.

through the columns of the *Daily Oregonian* and the weekly issues of *The New Northwest*."[66] The constant lobbying of women like Duniway irked at least one newspaper editor—Clarence Bagley—who stated in the *Puget Sound Weekly Courier* that "these women, utterly devoid of judgment or tact, with a sole desire for their own notoriety and aggrandizement, have made themselves a nuisance to members of almost every legislative meeting in Olympia since 1869."[67] ★ The 1883 suffrage bill simply amended Washington code with the language: "wherever the word 'his' occurs in the chapter aforesaid, it shall be construed to mean 'his' or 'her' as the case may be." The bill passed the house of representatives 14–9, with three absent. The legislative council voted 7–5 in favor of the legislation.[68] According to Duniway, "the Council had been thoroughly canvassed beforehand and no member offered to make a speech for or against it."[69] ★ Western suffrage historian T. Alfred Larson has analyzed the backgrounds of the 1883 legislators, arguing that farmers in the legislature were the primary supporters of women's suffrage. Larson

RESPECTFULLY DEDICATED TO LOYAL SUBJECTS OF LIBERTY

WHO PAVED THE WAY TO WOMAN'S ENFRANCHISEMENT IN THE PACIFIC NORTHWEST, UNITED STATES OF AMERICA, ANNO DOMINI ONE THOUSAND EIGHT HUNDRED EIGHTY THREE.

concluded that an agrarian background was the defining factor among pro-suffrage legislators—not marital status, foreign or native birth, age, or party affiliation.[70] Indeed, leadership for the bill came from agricultural eastern Washington. Some legislators, subscribing to the expediency argument, may have viewed women voters as a means to "purity, progress, and reform."[71] Another legislator, Representative Henry Miles, said 1883 was "a good time to try to experiment—if experiment it was—and if it proved a failure, it could be corrected when we become a state." Others thought the "absurd" legislation would bring notoriety on the legislature.[72] Only Wyoming and Utah territories had enacted woman's suffrage prior to this time. Washington's victory was different from those two territories, according to Larson, because women in Wyoming and Utah had not solicited the right to vote, while Washington's women petitioned and campaigned for the ballot.[73] ★ After the success of the suffrage bill, celebrations erupted around the state, but Olympia was the site of special jubilance. Duniway described the festivities in *The New Northwest*: ★ *It is 4 o'clock P.M. on Monday, November 19, 1883. As we write, church bells are ringing and a grand salute of minute guns sends out its joyful reverberations through the air proclaiming that Governor William A. Newell has formally announced that he will sign the Woman Suffrage bill and thereby make the women of Washington Territory free beyond peradventure . . . . All the people of Olympia . . . are rallying around the standard-bearers of liberty and justice, lifting their hearts and voices in unison with theirs to swell the glad anthem of rejoicing that ascend to heaven through the mingling hallelujahs of the guns and bells.*[74]

FACING PAGE: ABIGAIL SCOTT DUNIWAY DEVELOPED THIS POSTER IN TRIBUTE TO THE 1883 TERRITORIAL LEGISLATORS FOR PASSING A WOMEN'S SUFFRAGE BILL.

THIS PAGE: CLARA POTTLE SYLVESTER (1823–1906?) WAS A PROMINENT OLYMPIA SUFFRAGE ADVOCATE. A NATIVE OF DEER ISLE, MAINE, SHE CAME TO THE PACIFIC NORTHWEST IN 1854 WHEN SHE MARRIED EDMUND SYLVESTER, ONE OF OLYMPIA'S TOWN FATHERS.

In her account of the victory, Duniway recognized the many women of Olympia who supported the cause of suffrage, including sisters Emily Olney French and Mary Olney Brown, and Clara Sylvester, Ella Stork, and Janet Moore. It is no coincidence that many of these same women had been charter members of the first women's club on the West Coast, the Woman's Club of Olympia, which began meeting in 1883 at Sylvester's home. By one account, the club's purpose was to promote suffrage principles.[75] ★ Women's clubs offered a way to meet other like-minded individuals and gave women new to operating in the public sphere a place to gain experience and build confidence. ★ After the Civil War the movement gathered momentum nationally as an avenue for study and self-improvement. Historian Sandra Haarsager noted the differences for women's groups in the West, "The compression of time and the transient and unformed

ABBIE HOWARD HUNT STUART (1840?–1902) HELPED FOUND THE WOMAN'S CLUB OF OLYMPIA.

nature of the communities of the Pacific Northwest meant that their new clubs turned more quickly to meet immediate community needs . . . . Theirs was a bold attempt to aggregate and use power to order their world and create spaces for it for women inside and outside the club . . . ."[76] Historian Karen Blair notes that the women's clubs were important training grounds for suffragists. Through their club work women learned "to collect research, ask questions, refine viewpoints, form opinions, run committees, handle budgets, raise funds, circulate publicity, keep records, and lobby policy-makers: first for church, temperance, child-raising, literary societies, and social services; and [they] applied these lessons to their political work." ★ Although many organizations kept the issue in the background, pro-suffragists introduced their sister clubwomen to the cause.[77] Women uniting for change through clubs and organizations are a vital part of the struggle for equal rights in all eras in Washington history and reflect this western mindset.

Washington Women Organizing for Change

The influence of women joining together for mutual improvement and community benefit has been an important theme in Washington history, prefiguring the grassroots efforts of women during the suffrage campaigns and other reform efforts. Beginning in the 1830s, some of Washington's earliest Euro-American settlers were the wives of missionaries. Narcissa Whitman, Eliza Spalding, Myra Eels, Mary Richardson Walker, and Augusta Dix, for example, formed the Columbia Maternal Association in 1838—the first women's "club" in what was to become Washington.[78] ☆ Before the Civil War women nationwide participated in abolitionist, religious, and other reform-minded societies. During the war women in both North and South organized for relief on behalf of soldiers. Women in Vancouver, Washington, for example, formed the Vancouver Union Club, which eventually grew into a territory-wide effort. The combined contributions of many western Washington locales—raised through fairs, dances, and other events—totaled over $3,000 for the Union cause.[79] After the war women began to step out of the "domestic sphere" to participate in civic life. Susan B. Anthony worked with women and men to establish the Washington Territory Woman Suffrage Association in 1871, which endured throughout the tumultuous period of the women's suffrage campaign in territorial Washington. ☆ Inspired by their work in the Civil War era, women started study groups that met in their own homes or clubhouses. The Woman's Club of Olympia, organized in 1883 and still in existence, is recognized as one of the first study clubs on the West Coast and probably the first in Washington. According to one account, the club was founded to promote suffrage principles.[80] In fact, Abigail Scott Duniway credited club founder Abbie Hunt Stuart with recognizing that the 1883 suffrage victory could be short-lived (as it was) and that initiating the women's club movement in Washington could provide an organizational base and experience for women

campaigning for suffrage. After her success in organizing the Olympia club, Stuart went to Portland in 1894 to initiate the club movement in Oregon.[81] ☆ Women of all races and backgrounds organized clubs to advocate for their own issues and concerns. Many Washington women's clubs affiliated in 1896 as the General Federation of Women's Clubs. Although the federation did not endorse women's right to vote in Washington, club women were the backbone of the suffrage movement. Women's clubs steered away from self-improvement to "municipal housekeeping" after the turn of the twentieth century—seeing their club work as an extension of their own home responsibilities. However, women seeking change saw that, without the right to vote, they could do little more than advocate for their cause. ☆ Starting in 1906 Emma Smith DeVoe organized suffrage clubs throughout the state, often calling on clubwomen for assistance. According to historian Sandra Haarsager, Seattleite Nellie Fick called together a meeting of prominent clubwomen in her home in 1908 to form the Seattle Suffrage Club. Carrie Chapman Catt named Fick to represent Washington in the national campaign. Other clubwomen joined the suffrage cause in 1909, including Carrie Hill, founder of the Woman's Century Club and the Seattle Women's Industrial Club.[82] To conduct the 1909–1910 campaign women organized through the Washington Equal Suffrage Association, the Washington Political Equality League, Seattle's Alki Suffrage Club, and myriad local organizations. The WCTU played

Page(s) from the History of the Woman's Century Club of Seattle, *established in 1891. Carrie Chapman Catt was the club's first president.*

an important role in advocating for suffrage and the enactment of prohibition in Washington. ✫ Armed with the right to vote, clubwomen were potent legislative advocates for mothers' pensions and other reforms. During World War I clubwomen actively assisted in the war effort. During this period a coalition of women's clubs and working-

class women effectively pursued reform.[83] The coalition dissolved when these two groups clashed over radicalism and patriotism before and during World War I. ✫ By the mid 1920s, according to historian Karen Blair, the club movement began to stall as young women found opportunities for social and political engagement elsewhere.[84] Enfranchised women, however, continued to lobby for change, often concentrating their efforts around such interests as pro- or anti-feminist causes, political parties, hobbies, historical societies, and professional organizations. ✫ African American women joined together in cities and towns all over Washington to form clubs for self-improvement and civic betterment. The first clubs took root in Washington cities during the early days of statehood—e.g., the Colored Ladies' Society organized in Seattle in late 1889. African American women established the Historical and Scientific Club (including men) and Pierian Literary Club in Spokane. Susie Revels Cayton and others, including chiropodist Dr. Letitia Denny Graves, established the Dorcas Charity Club in Seattle in 1906. Nettie Asberry initiated the Tuesday Art Club in Tacoma, and a group of Everett women formed the Nannie Burroughs Study Club, named for an African American educator. ✫ During World War I African American women in cities like Seattle formed their own unofficial units of the Red Cross. Alice Fields worked with the Red Cross and King County Minute Women. Black women provided home-front war support by participating in knitting groups, including one in Roslyn, to make knitted garments for American soldiers. By 1917 the Washington State Association of Colored Women's Clubs had been established, with branches in Seattle, Tacoma, Everett, and Vancouver. The Seattle group purchased a large house in 1923 where classes for women were held and where newcomers to the city could find temporary lodging. During the 1970s and 1980s the Seattle Cosmopolitan Century Club operated a viewing room on one floor of their clubhouse. The Northwest African American Museum and Black Historical Society now possess records of many of these organizations.[85] ✫ Signaling changes in the numbers of educated and professional women in the state, the American Association of University Women (1927) and Business and Professional Women (1920) formed in Washington. Latina, black, Native American, and Asian women all created organizations that served their interests and culture, including the American Indian Women's Service League (1958), Washington State Association of Colored Women's Clubs, (1917), El Centro de la Raza, (1972), and Chong Wa Benevolent Association (1915). Campfire Girls, Girl Scouts, 4-H, and other clubs devoted to young women continue to flourish.

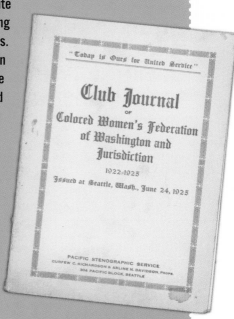

Above, left: Built in 1908, the Woman's Club of Olympia clubhouse is now listed on the national, state, and Olympia heritage registers.

Above, right: Published by the Pacific Stenographic Service, the Club Journal *included photographs of prominent African American club leaders and descriptions of individuals and events.*

Washington's Early Women's Clubs

1838: Columbia Maternal Association, wives of Presbyterian missionaries discussed child raising.

1880s: Northwest churches commonly formed ladies aid societies and missionary support groups.

1883: Women's Christian Temperance Union came to Seattle and expanded rapidly. By 1890, there were 885 members in Washington.

1883: Woman's Club of Olympia founded. It built a clubhouse in Olympia that is still standing.

1886: Seattle Children's Home, an orphanage, founded. Ladies guilds throughout the state raised money to support the institution.

1889: Colored Ladies Society (also known as Ladies' Colored Social Circle) founded in Seattle.

1890: Seattle Ladies Musical Club established.

1891: Spokane Sorosis founded.

1891: New normal schools formed in Ellensburg and Cheney to train teachers. Literary societies and YWCA clubs are encouraged for extracurricular activities.

1891: Aloha Club founded in Tacoma.

1891: New Century Club forms in Seattle. It would build a clubhouse that still stands, as Harvard Exit Theatre. Among early members was Carrie Chapman (Catt), who became the national leader of the fight for women's suffrage.

1892: Cultus Club founded in Spokane.

1894: Everett Book Club founded.

1894: Society of Literary Explorers, Port Townsend, founded.

1894: Woman's Club of Yakima founded; clubhouse stands today.

1894: Woman's Reading Club, Walla Walla, founded.

1894: Hoquiam Woman's Literary Club founded.

1895: Chehalis St. Helena Club established.

1895: Woman's Industrial Club founded for self-supporting women.

1895: Centralia Ladies of the Round Table organized.

1895: Friday Club founded in Ellensburg, Washington.

1896: Woman's Club of Snohomish founded.

1896: The first chapter of PEO founded in Seattle.

1896: Tacoma women call for the founding of a Washington State Federation of Women's Clubs to unite the members of all state clubs. The following year, its first annual convention is held in Olympia.

Early twentieth century: Consumer's League investigates businesses for fair labor practices. Women members promise to frequent approved establishments for goods and services.

1900: Seattle branch of the National Council of Jewish Women founded.

1905: Jewish women's club founded a settlement house for immigrants.

1906: Dorcas Charity Club founded by black women for foster home.

1907: Women's guilds form to help raise funds for Children's Orthopedic Hospital, founded by Anna Clise.

1907: Bellingham YWCA founded.

Compiled by Dr. Karen Blair from: Jane Cunningham Croly, *The History of the Woman's Club Movement in America*; Sandra Haarsager, *Organized Womanhood: Cultural Politics in the Pacific Northwest, 1840–1920*; Mildred Andrews, *Washington Women as Path Breakers*; Mildred Andrews, *Woman's Place: A Guide to Seattle and King County History*; Dana Frank, *Purchasing Power: Consumer Organizing, Gender, and the Seattle Labor Movement, 1919–1929*. See also: Dr. Karen J. Blair, *The Clubwoman as Feminist: True Womanhood Redefined, 1868–1914* (New York: Holmes and Meier Publishers, Inc., 1980); Dr. Karen J. Blair, "The History of Women's Clubs" (Washington State History Museum, Tacoma, March 29, 2007), http://www.washingtonwomenshistory.org/themes/clubs/historyOfClubsBlairAudio.aspx.

Women Exercise the Right to Vote

Although newspaper editor C. B. Bagley held high expectations for women voters, he cautioned that suffrage was "now on trial."[86] Women did uphold expectations, for example, voting in greater proportion to their number than men in 1884 when they cast 12,000 out of 48,000 ballots.[87] In June 1884 Seattle women turned out in force for the so-called outdoor Apple Orchard Convention held at

Fourth and Marion, when the Law and Order League rallied for the moral cleanup of Seattle. Later, 759 registered women helped vote out a corrupt administration at the July election.[88] The *Seattle Mirror* said of the Seattle municipal election, "It was the first election in the city where the women could vote, and the first where the gambling and liquor fraternity, which had so long controlled the municipal government to an enormous extent, suffered defeat."[89] Women voters in Olympia likewise helped turn back corrupt officials. Of the November 1884 general election, the *Olympia Transcript* reported: "The result shows that all parties must put up good men if they expect to elect them. They can not do as they have in the past—nominate any candidates, and elect them by the force of the party lash."[90] Cornelia Jenner, an advocate for reform of Seattle politics, described what it was like for women to vote in the election of 1884:

> I went in company with Mrs. Thomas and Mrs. Smith as early as possible this morning (between nine and ten o'clock) down to the voting place of the terrible First Ward, and remained except during lunch, until seven o'clock this evening.... We have no cause to complain as regards our treatment; policy and police, made men respectful. I only heard three oaths, those not the most blasphemous.[91]

Demonstrating their effectiveness in 1884, women voters helped elect Charles S. Voorhees of Colfax as delegate to Congress, the first Washington Democrat since the Civil War. This victory caused consternation among many male voters in the generally Republican Washington Territory. In 1886, Voorhees ran for Congress again, this time opposed by Republican Charles M. Bradshaw, a Port Townsend lawyer. For many years, Bradshaw had lived with but had not married a Native American woman, with whom he had children. Voorhees's victory over Bradshaw may have happened because women objected to his domestic arrangements. According to attorney and historian Charles Wiggins, this hard-fought partisan victory may have influenced Republicans to line up against women's suffrage in the state constitution vote in 1889.[92]

UPPER: OCTOBER 1884 BROADSIDE FROM TACOMA SOLICITING MEN AND WOMEN VOTERS' PARTICIPATION IN A SCHOOL BOARD ELECTION.

LOWER: AN ACTIVE WOMEN'S CHRISTIAN TEMPERANCE MOVEMENT MEMBER AND A SUFFRAGIST, CORNELIA EXPERIENCE COMSTOCK JENNER (1846-1891) CAME TO SEATTLE FROM TIOGA COUNTY, NEW YORK, VIA CALIFORNIA.

Challenges to the Suffrage Law

Women's right to vote aroused strong opponents. Made legal householders by the legislature in 1881 and voters under the 1883 suffrage law, women became qualified jurors. Female jury service precipitated the first judicial challenge to the 1883 suffrage legislation. In 1884, Molly Rosencrantz was accused of keeping a house of prostitution in Tacoma and was indicted by a grand jury of five women and one man. A motion was made to set the indictment aside, calling the grand jury invalid because women served on the panel. Rosencrantz was later convicted. On appeal before the Territorial Supreme Court, Justices John P. Hoyt and S. C. Wingard determined that territorial law did indeed properly define women as householders and voters—the two criteria for jury service.[93] Justice George Turner dissented. A Missouri native, Turner had been appointed to the Washington Territorial bench in 1884 by President Chester Arthur as a party-loyalist Republican lawyer from Alabama.[94]

Turner opined in his dissent that "legislative enactment would not make white black, nor can it provide the female form with bone and sinew equal in strength to that with which nature had provided man. No more can it reverse the law of cause and effect, and clothe a timid, shrinking woman, whose life theater is and will continue to be and ought to continue to be primarily the home circle, with the masculine will and self-reliant judgment of man."[95]

Elected in part by women, the 1885–1886 legislature enacted alcohol education laws and local-option prohibition, which generated alarm among the saloon lobby.[96] Duniway recognized the danger of the anti-liquor legislation to the future of female suffrage in Washington. She knew that when local-option laws for prohibition succeeded, it was frequently blamed on the so-called women's vote. By 1886, Duniway began speaking against local-option prohibition, but churches and the Woman's Christian Temperance Union (WCTU) shunned her.

Perhaps spurred by the Rosencrantz case, the 1886 legislature amended the original 1883 act to state clearly that "all American citizens, male and female" could vote, rather than the vague wording of 1883 legislation, which stipulated that where *his* was used in law, it was to be construed as *his* and *her*. Briefly before final passage, the bill had included the provision that all voters were entitled to hold office, but that was hastily reversed. Governor Watson Squire signed the legislation on November 26, 1886.[97]

In 1887 the Territorial Supreme Court again focused on the legality of women's suffrage.

which they had made decisions at the trial court level were appealed to the Supreme Court.) In his decision, Turner again waxed eloquent about the proper sphere of women, which, he argued, was removed from civic life.[99] The *Tacoma Ledger* questioned how the decision could have been written so quickly, noting "the opinion of Judges Turner and Langford on wiping out woman suffrage in Washington Territory contains 15,000 words. Does any sensible man or woman in the Territory believe that it was prepared between Monday afternoon, when the case was argued, and Thursday morning when it was given to the public? This fact makes it look like a conspiracy more than ever."[100]

After the Supreme Court decision, a group of thirty-six Seattle women signed a petition to Congress written by Seattle legislator and lawyer John Kinnear asking that the suffrage laws be revalidated. [101] The women stated their cause at an indignation meeting:

Indicted by a grand jury that included women, Tacoma gambler Jeff Harland appealed his conviction on the basis that women were not legal jurors. Harland's appeal was likely a test case pushed by liquor interests to disenfranchise women and supported by the notorious Harry Morgan, a Tacoma saloon and gambling figure known as a "boss sport"—a person associated with illicit activities."[98] The court sided with Harland, determining that the title of the 1883 law did not describe the content of the legislative act, making it invalid along with the provisions of the 1886 amendment. The justices ruled that because the 1883 act was invalid, women were not qualified electors and thus not legal jurors.

Justice Turner, again showing his anti-suffrage bias, wrote the majority opinion in the Harland case. Despite the fact that nineteen other laws passed in the 1883 session were lacking a similar descriptive title, the court backed Harland, with Justice William Langford concurring with Turner and Justice Roger Greene dissenting. Another jurist, Justice John P. Hoyt was disqualified from weighing in since he had heard the case in the trial court. (At that time, Supreme Court judges also acted as trial judges and had to recuse themselves if the cases on

We are disenfranchised; stripped of our rights and our liberties, and reduced to equality with the squalid savage and the heathen Chinese. We have met to take steps to regain our rights. We are the beacon lights of this movement, and were progressing satisfactorily when this severe blow came upon us. All the more severe because we had tasted the sweets of liberty. We are disenfranchised, and we can weep, wail, and gnash our teeth, and our prayers will avail us nothing against those two old sticklers on law, but we can make ourselves felt in other ways. I suggest that we at once petition the President to remove these two old fossils—those two old carpet baggers, (applause) and ask him to appoint citizens of this Territory in their places. Voorhees was elected by the votes of women and if he has any gallantry, he will do all in his power to get Congress to give us back our rights. The case looked pretty bad at first, but at second thought it is more hopeful. If the question comes to a vote of the people we can get the votes of the 14,000 women who voted at the last election, and the votes of the 8,000 Knights of Labor, besides many liberal-minded person's votes, thus giving us a majority of the 41,000 votes in the Territory.[102]

THIS PAGE: SPOKANE FALLS BOARD OF TRADE TELEGRAM TO D. M. DRUMHELLER, DATED JANUARY 17, 1888. PEOPLE ON BOTH SIDES OF THE RE-ENACTED SUFFRAGE BILL LOBBIED GOVERNOR EUGENE SEMPLE BEFORE HE SIGNED IT INTO LAW. SOME FELT THAT GIVING WOMEN THE VOTE WOULD THWART WASHINGTON'S STATEHOOD AMBITIONS.

FACING PAGE: TACOMA MAYOR JACOB ROBERT WEISBACH AND A COMMITTEE COMPOSED MAINLY OF LOCAL BUSINESS OWNERS FORCED CHINESE RESIDENTS TO LEAVE TOWN IN NOVEMBER 1885.

Both radical women associated with the Knights of Labor as well as members of more conservative groups, such as the WCTU, joined the protest.[103] The suffrage cause appealed to the Knights of Labor and other labor groups, who believed white workers should have preference over immigrants, especially the Chinese, and that white women voters would support that cause. White middle-class women, for their part, furthered the idea of their moral and cultural superiority in making their case for voting rights.[104] These two groups—white middle-class women and labor—would eventually join with the Populists for the 1898 suffrage campaign and with Progressives for success in 1910.

After the judicial decision overturning women's right to vote, suffragists descended on the legislature once again, and on January 18, 1888, legislators reenacted a women's suffrage law with the appropriate title. However, this version of the law excluded women from jury service, perhaps to circumvent contested legal issues like those in the Rosencrantz and Harland cases. Deluged with letters and petitions on both sides of the issue, some, including Seattle judge and civic promoter Thomas Burke, urged Governor Eugene Semple not to sign the measure, fearing women's suffrage was a radical measure that would imperil the Washington's chances for statehood. Semple ultimately signed the legislation but said little about the issue himself.[105] National suffragists, including Lucy Stone, along with temperance and labor groups praised Semple's action.

The suffrage victory was short-lived. In April 1888, Spokane city election judges accepted other women's votes, but one judge—John A. Todd—rejected the ballot of Nevada Bloomer, wife of a saloon owner. Todd, who supplied liquor to the Bloomer's tavern, was part of the lobby that feared women would vote for prohibition.[106] A trial court agreed with Todd, but Bloomer appealed to the Territorial Supreme Court.

THE
Chinese Must Go!

Mayor Weisbach
Has called a MASS MEETING for this (Saturday) evening at 7:30 o'clock
AT ALPHA OPERA HOUSE.
To consider the Chinese question.

TURN OUT.

Once again, George Turner, then retired from the Supreme Court, played a pivotal role in the decision by advocating a new anti-suffrage argument. Representing the election officials, he argued before the court that the federal government had intended to put the word *male* before *citizenship* in the Washington Territorial Organic Act when establishing voter qualifications. Deciding the case in August 1888, Justices Richard Jones, William Langford, and Frank Allyn agreed with Turner that the 1888 legislation was invalid. They explained that when the Washington Territorial Organic Act passed Congress, "the word 'citizen' was used as a qualification for voting and holding office and, in our judgment, the word then meant and still signifies male citizenship and must be so construed."[107] Suffragists raised $5,000 to appeal the case to the U.S. Supreme Court, but by the time it reached the docket in 1891 the lawyers had agreed to dismiss the case.[108] Some members of Congress believed that the court decision had cheated Washington women out of the ballot. Maine's Republican senator, George Hoar, for example, proposed that women should be able to vote for delegates and participate in the 1889 Constitutional Convention.[109]

The failure to carry the Bloomer case to the Supreme Court can be blamed not only on anti-prohibitionists but also, according to Seattle historian Clarence Bagley, on the response of the law-and-order men in Seattle to the "ill-advised actions" of women in the city during the Chinese "troubles" of 1885 and 1886.[110] The high turnout of working-class women at the 1886 elections and their participation in the anti-Chinese rioting upset the businessmen who felt tumult surrounding Chinese expulsion might undermine the chances for statehood.[111]

Although Bagley called the actions "troubles," they were far more than that for the Chinese. Nation-

ally, opposition to Chinese labor had been formalized with enactment of the federal Chinese Exclusion Act of 1882, which restricted immigration and access to citizenship. Large numbers of Chinese laborers had come to Washington to work on railroad construction and in other industries, triggering prejudice among whites. Labor organizations (dominated by whites) saw the Chinese as competition for scarce jobs.

The situation reached a boiling point when in November 1885 a Tacoma mob drove Chinese residents out of the city; in Seattle a few months later the Knights of Labor led the violence, hounding Chinese out of town. Although some officials tried to deter the violence, most Chinese fled. Seattle socialist Mary Kenworthy was a key connection between suffragists and anti-Chinese forces. She was elected president of the King County Equal Suffrage League in 1883 and became a leader in the Chinese expulsion. Although Kenworthy was later tried and acquitted for her part in the riot, her actions seemed to symbolize a lawlessness that told the nation Washington Territory might not be ready for statehood.[112]

After the Bloomer case, according to Seattle suffragist Adella Parker, "the women were begged not to start a new legal action and all were eager for admission to the Union. Furthermore, the women were assured that if they would trust to the chivalry of the men, suffrage would be incorporated into the new constitution."[113] Parker was a Seattle high school teacher, Progressive activist, and graduate of the University of Washington Law School who would play a major role in the 1909–1910 suffrage campaign as head of the College Equal Suffrage League in western Washington.[114]

Women's suffrage was not the only reform Washington's conservative Territorial Supreme Court targeted during the period. The court also overturned

To The Honorable:

The President and Delegates representing the people of Washington in Constitutional Convention on July 4th, 1889, assembled for the purpose of forming a Constitution for the New State of Washington:

Your petitioners, the undersigned would respectfully petition:—That in the Constitution framed by your Honorable Body there be included such provisions as shall secure to women in the future State of Washington, the exercise of the right of suffrage to the same extent and upon the same basis as men.

local-option prohibition in 1888, although a modified local-option law was later reenacted.[115] Conservative court decisions like these spurred the independent Populist and Progressive movements in Washington over the course of the next two decades and created the political climate in which women were eventually successful in achieving permanent voting rights.

Suffrage and Statehood

Only male voters selected the members of Washington's second Constitutional Convention, which began in Olympia on July 4, 1889, and the suffrage cause was weakened correspondingly. Parker said that Henry Blackwell, an AWSA representative who attended the convention, found that only two of seventy-five delegates were in favor of women's suffrage.[116] Reacting to those who opposed suffrage, the revitalized Equal Suffrage League (ESL) [117] met in Olympia. A resolution passed by its members declared that three successive territorial legislative assemblies had enacted suffrage while it decried the fact that delegates to the convention did not represent the 20,000 women of Washington.

Suffragists "flooded" the convention with petitions.[118] They hoped long-time suffrage advocate Edward Eldridge would head the Elections and Elective Rights Committee. Although Eldridge had been a delegate to the 1878 constitutional convention and was a delegate again in 1889, P. C. Sullivan, a Republican lawyer from Tacoma, chaired the elections committee. Suffrage opponent George Turner headed the judiciary committee, and John P. Hoyt chaired the convention. As a Washington Territory supreme court justice, Hoyt had voted with the majority in upholding women's right to vote in 1884 and favored a direct vote of the people on the suffrage issue, but he reportedly secured his position as chair of the convention by agreeing to limit prosuffrage committee chairs.[119]

Eldridge spoke eloquently when the voting article came before the entire convention on August 12,

1889, moving to strike the word *male* from the voting section. Debates followed about whether women's right to vote should be decided by the legislature or by a vote of the people. Proposals that women be allowed to vote in municipal elections, that women themselves vote on the issue of suffrage, and that women be able to hold public office were all defeated. Some delegates wanted a vote on the suffrage issue when prohibition was not on the ticket at the same time. Eldridge also proposed continuing territory-wide ballots on the issue. These efforts all failed.

Although elections committee chairman P. C. Sullivan initially extended him an invitation, delegates denied Henry Blackwell the opportunity to speak directly to the gathering. Not surprisingly, George Turner dissuaded his colleagues from hosting the distinguished suffrage leader.[120] Blackwell spoke instead at Olympia's Tacoma Hall, urging convention members to keep the word *male* out of the constitution, and he presented supporting letters from officials in territories where women had the vote. Becoming dispirited afterwards, he wrote, "Here I am fighting against odds—both the party conventions & leaders having dropped woman suffrage in order to conciliate the whiskey interest & the very general opposition which the men have manifested since the judges have overthrown the women's right of suffrage. It is a most discouraging & perplexing condition of things."[121]

Another national figure, suffragist and newspaper editor Clara Bewick Colby, traveled around Washington during 1889. She published accounts of the trip in her paper, *The Woman's Tribune*, beginning in April of that year. Colby supported state advocates and

FACING PAGE: ARDENT SUFFRAGIST ADELLA PARKER WAS ONE OF THE EDITORS OF THE CAMPAIGN JOURNAL *VOTES FOR WOMEN*.

THIS PAGE: SUFFRAGISTS SUBMITTED PETITIONS IN FAVOR OF WOMEN'S VOTING RIGHTS TO THE 1889 STATE CONSTITUTIONAL CONVENTION, WITHOUT SUCCESS.

WASHINGTON WOMEN'S COOK BOOK.

Election October 1st, 1889.

For Representative to 51st Congress
JOHN L. WILSON
For Governor
ELISHA P FERRY
For Lieutenant Governor
CHARLES E. LAUGHTON.
For Secretary of State
ALLEN WEIR
For State Treasurer
ADDISON A LINDSLEY
For State Auditor.
THOMAS M REED
For Attorney General.
WILLIAM C. JONES.
For Superintendent of Public Instruction:
ROBERT B. BRYAN
For Commissioner of Public Lands·
WILLIAM T FORREST
For Judges of the Supreme Court
RALPH O DUNBAR.
THEODORE L STILES,
JOHN P HOYT,
THOMAS J. ANDERS,
ELMON SCOTT
FIRST—For the Constitution
Against the Constitution.
SECOND—For Woman Suffrage.
Against Woman Suffrage.
THIRD—For Prohibition.
Against Prohibition
FOURTH—For the Permanent Location of
the Seat of Government

———

King County Republican Ticket.

For Judge of the Superior Court,
JULIUS A STRATTON
For County Clerk.
M M HOLMES

Legislative Ticket.

For State Senators 19th Senatorial District,
W D WOOD,
J H. JONES,
O D GUILFOIL,
J R KINNEAR,
W V RINEHART.
For Representatives King County,
J. T BLACKBURN,
W C RUTTER,
W. H HUGHES,
ALEXANDER ALLEN
W. J. SHINN,
GEO. BOTHELL,
F. W BIRD,
FRED J GRANT.

traveled widely to meet with interested groups and help establish new suffrage organizations. Suffragist lecturer Matilda Hindman of Pennsylvania and California attorney and speaker Laura de Force Gordon joined Colby in canvassing Washington. Colby also worked extensively with ministers and local wCTU members to pressure delegates.[122]

Despite these efforts, the constitutional convention delegates decided that women's suffrage would be a separate issue on the statewide ballot, along with adoption of the proposed constitution itself and separate tallies on the location of the capital and enactment of prohibition. By and large the framers considered that women's support for prohibition and their tendency to vote as independents constituted a threat to Washington's party-based environment. According to the *History of Woman Suffrage,* one politician said, "Women are natural mugwumps, and I hate a mugwump"—i.e., an independent-minded reformer.[123]

Colby gave this advice to Washington women who went to the polls on election day:

> *Every community should be thoroughly canvassed so as to ensure the presence of a large body of women. The front of a store or some building or both should be engaged on both sides of the polls so that no man may escape importunity. The places where the women congregate, and, if permission is given, the polling places themselves should be decorated with flags and emblems. Mottoes embodying the plea and the principle will readily suggest themselves. Hot coffee and a tempting lunch should be served for the efficiency of such measures is proverbial.*[124]

Defiantly, the Equal Suffrage League urged women to exercise their former rights by going to the polls and voting on the ratification of the constitution and the suffrage article. The league reasoned that these ballots could be classified as "rejected" and set aside for a possible U.S. Supreme Court test case. However, even if the women's votes had been counted, the suffrage article likely would not have passed.[125] While the state constitution was ratified on October 1, 1889, by a territory-wide vote, the separate suffrage proposal lost by 19,000 votes, 16,521–35,913. Prohibition also failed, 19,546–31,487.

Men's failure in 1889 to vote for suffrage just one year after legislative enactment of women's right to vote is puzzling. Legal historian Sandra Van Burkleo theorizes that male voters voted down suffrage because they were uncomfortable with the heightened status accorded to women created by the vote—jury service, public participation, and status out of the domestic sphere.[126] The 1889 State Constitution established the electorate as:

> All male persons of the age of twenty-one years or over, possessing the following qualifications, shall be entitled to vote at all elections: They shall be citizens of the United States; They shall have lived in the state one year, and in the county ninety days, and in the city, town, ward, or precinct thirty days immediately preceding the election at which they offer to vote; Provided, that Indians not taxed shall never be allowed the elective franchise; Provided, further, that all male persons who at the time of the adoption of this Constitution are qualified electors of the Territory, shall be electors.

After statehood, enacting women's suffrage in Washington required both a two-thirds majority legislative approval and a statewide election plural-ity to amend the constitution—a more difficult task than in territorial times when only legislative action was required.

Adella Parker claimed there was a conspiracy among liquor interests to defeat the women's suffrage measure in 1889. She believed liquor wholesalers had preprinted Republican Party ballots—ironically, at a print shop for a temperance publication. Before Washington statehood and the requirement of the Australian or secret ballot, each party printed its own ballots and distributed them for use at the polls. Parker, to prove her point, printed an example of the altered ballot in her article in the 1909 *Washington Women's Cook Book*. The ballot shows both "For Woman Suffrage" and "Against the Constitution" marked out. Parker claimed that 180,000 bogus ballots were printed, which she called "vest pocket votes for the liquor interests." She noted that a change of just one vote in twelve would have carried women's suffrage.[127]

Washington joined the union on November 11, 1889. The next year, the state legislature authorized women to vote for local school trustees and directors but not for county or state school superintendents. Although partial suffrage was more empowering than no vote at all, without full suffrage women possessed only selective voting rights without being full democratic participants.

The 1890 legislature opened all types of employment to women except public office.[128] Ella Guptill challenged the law. After she was elected superintendent of schools in Clallam County in 1894, her male opponent contested her victory because she was a woman. Guptill lobbied the legislature for a change in the law, and in 1895 lawmakers authorized women to hold school board, state board of education, and school superintendent offices.[129] By 1900 seven counties had elected women as school superintendents, which reflected the preponderance of women amongst professional educators in the state—2,288 women to 1,033 men.[130]

FACING PAGE, LEFT: IN 1889 EACH POLITICAL PARTY PRINTED AND DISTRIBUTED ITS OWN BALLOTS. AS MANY AS 180,000 FRAUDULENT BALLOTS WERE PREPRINTED WITH A VOTE AGAINST WOMEN'S SUFFRAGE. ONE SUFFRAGIST CALLED THESE "VEST POCKET VOTES FOR THE LIQUOR INTERESTS."

FACING PAGE, RIGHT: CLARA BEWICK COLBY (1846-1916) TRAVELED AROUND WASHINGTON DURING THE 1889 SUFFRAGE CAMPAIGN AND PUBLISHED ACCOUNTS OF THE TRIP IN HER NEWSPAPER, *THE WOMAN'S TRIBUNE.*

THIS PAGE: ELLA GUPTILL (1870-1943) TAUGHT AT THE PUGET SOUND COOPERATIVE COLONY IN PORT ANGELES BEFORE BEING ELECTED CLALLAM COUNTY SCHOOL SUPERINTENDENT IN 1894.

Women Vote for State Flower

While the (male) voters of the state did not believe that women should have the franchise except in school elections, women alone voted for the state flower. The issue arose when Washington was invited to participate in the 1893 Chicago Columbian Exposition and part of each state's exposition display was to be a flower representing the state. Washington did not have an official flower, and the Washington State Fair Committee left the matter to its female members. Historian Karen Blair has noted that their interest arose from a sense of state patriotism and loyalty of the time and reflected the role of women—especially clubwomen—in advocating for beautification and environmentalism.[131]

The flower election was spirited. Ella Higginson, the state poet laureate from Bellingham, wrote a widely published poem about the four-leaf clover. The *Spokane Review* thought the fleur-de-lis was a good alternative. Others suggested the dogwood, gaillardia, syringa, wild rose, marguerite, and Oregon grape. In February 1892 Alsora Hayner Fry, a transplanted New Yorker, suggested in a letter to a Seattle newspaper that the rhododendron should be the state flower. One Seattle woman responded that the rhododendron was not native to Washington, and Bellingham papers noted it was already the state flower of West Virginia.

Polling places for women voting in the flower election included post offices, which displayed the request, "Would you kindly see that every lady coming in has the privilege of signing her name for preference of the state flower?" Fry's campaign headquarters at Lee's drugstore at Second and Columbia in Seattle featured art exhibits and flower displays. She even put clover in the window and had rabbits on hand to eat the display. Balloting closed August 1, 1892, and the rhododendron won over clover 7,704–5,720 out of 14,419 votes cast. The Washington State Senate confirmed the rhododendron on February 10, 1893.[132] Apparently resigned to its success, Higginson eventually also wrote a poem about the rhododendron. Despite the 1893 vote, the

Jury Service

The 1911 Washington State Legislature specified that all electors, including women, would be eligible jurors—finally settling the issue that precipitated the court cases overturning women's suffrage in the 1880s. Washington became the first state in the union to legislate authorization for women to serve as jurors. The statute did allow a sex-based exemption, however, since women could opt out of jury duty without cause. This exemption was removed by state law in 1967, and the current law (RCW 2.36.030(3))—enacted in 1979—states that "a citizen shall not be excluded from jury service in this state on account of race, color, religion, sex, national origin, or economic status."[133]

rhododendron did not officially become the state flower until 1949, when both houses of the legislature confirmed it. In 1959 the legislature further defined the state flower as *Rhododendron macrophyllum*, native to western North America, which continues to represent Washington today.

The Suffrage Fight Resumes

*D*uring the early 1890s farmers' groups and labor unions—notably the Knights of Labor—united to form the Populist movement, responding to economic hard times. Populists in Washington wanted changes in government, including regulation of railroads, reduction of taxes, direct election of federal senators, and citizen control of government. This new movement boded well for another suffrage vote because farmers' groups had traditionally favored it. The Washington State Grange had been pro-women's suffrage from its inception in 1889 and farmer-legislators had taken the lead in enacting suffrage during the territorial period. The Knights of Labor's support of the suffrage movement was based on the belief that white women would protect white men's jobs.

Although a nominal state suffrage organization continued in existence throughout the 1890s, women's suffrage legislation was not introduced in any legislative session between 1889 and 1894.[134] Despite the natural affinity between Populism and women's suffrage, Washington Populists did not include women's suffrage in their platform until 1895, several years after their founding in 1891. Seeing the strength of Populism in the state, Washington suffragists looked to other western states for models of Populist-backed suffrage victories. Populist coalitions in Colorado in 1893 and in Idaho in 1896 backed successful constitutional amendments for women's suffrage. They formed a western quartet of voting states after Utah enacted women's suffrage as part of the

new state constitution in 1896, reflecting Utah's long history of women's suffrage dating from 1870. Wyoming, the first territory to enact women's right to vote in 1869, had entered the union in 1890 as a suffrage state.[135]

In 1895 Washington Populists joined with reformist Republican legislators in supporting women's suffrage legislation. Populist leaders Representative John R. Rogers from Puyallup and Representative S. W. Fenton from Thurston County presented petitions to the legislature supporting the measure. After a victory in the state senate, the house narrowly defeated women's suffrage—falling short of the necessary two-thirds majority.

Besides failing to enact women's suffrage legislation, the 1895 legislature moved to amend the constitution to further restrict voter qualifications by requiring that electors be able to read and speak English. Voters approved the amendment in a statewide vote in 1896. (This voter qualification continued when women eventually secured the right to vote in 1910.)[136] The enactment of this voting restriction was a response to growing nativist opposition to immigration. Nativists blamed Washington's widespread depression of 1893 on low-paid immigrant workers and foreign actions. At this time 20 percent of Washington's population was foreign-born.[137] Not until 1974 was a literacy requirement expunged from Washington's constitution.

After the narrow legislative defeat in 1896, women's suffrage again seemed a possibility if given strong support from various reformist political groups. Populists had gained political traction in Washington while the issue of free silver united several parties and

FACING PAGE, LEFT: ELSORA HAYNER FRY (D. 1926) CHAMPIONED THE RHODODENDRON FOR STATE FLOWER.

FACING PAGE, RIGHT: ELSORA HAYNER FRY'S RHODODENDRON DRESS, WHICH SHE WORE TO THE STATE BALL IN OLYMPIA IN 1893.

THIS PAGE: LAURA HALL PETERS (1840-1902)—AN ADVOCATE FOR TEMPERANCE, SUFFRAGE, ANTI-CHINESE AGITATION WITH THE KNIGHTS OF LABOR, UTOPIANISM, AND POPULISM—SHEPHERDED THE 1897 SUFFRAGE BILL THROUGH THE STATE LEGISLATURE.

factions—including Populists, Silver Republicans,[138] and Democrats—against regular Republicans. Silver Republicans, and the Prohibition, Social Democratic, and Socialist Labor parties all endorsed women's suffrage without significant opposition from Democrats and Republicans.[139] In 1896 the Populist Party platform unequivocally demanded "enactment into law the following propositions: . . . that the next legislature take the necessary steps to submit to the electors of this state to be voted upon at the next regular election an amendment to the state constitution conferring the elective franchise upon women citizens of this state."[140]

The Fusion Party (Silver Republicans, Democrats, and Populists) gained legislative seats in 1896, providing a positive political climate for women's suffrage in the legislature. Laura Hall Peters, an advocate for a variety of causes—including temperance,

suffrage, anti-Chinese agitation with the Knights of Labor, utopianism, and Populism—managed the bill.[141] Representative James P. de Mattos, a Silver Republican from Whatcom County, championed the legislation since he credited his success in public office during the 1880s to women voters in Bellingham. Populists and Silver Republicans in the house and senate supported the bill using arguments of equal rights, reform, and the desire to refer the issue to the electorate for a final determination—all doctrines of Populism.

The house voted in favor of the women's suffrage bill 54–15 in early February. The senate amended the bill and passed it in late February 23–11. The house failed to take up the revised measure until the last day before the end of the session, and Peters orchestrated the final legislative action.[142] Although about fifty women were present when the bill passed the senate, lobbying had been limited. A description by Peters of anti-suffrage forces' last-minute attempt to derail the bill is recorded in the *History of Woman Suffrage*. When Senator Thomas Miller happened to examine the bill that had finally passed the house, he noticed that it had been mysteriously replaced with a bogus document, apparently by anti-suffragists. Peters personally carried the correct bill to Governor John R. Rogers for his signature.[143] After Governor Rogers signed the bill, the amendment was sent to Washington's (male) voters in November 1898. The road for suffragists was never easy; roadblocks arose from many directions—including their own strategies, which proved ineffective in 1898.

The Washington Equal Suffrage Association (WESA) did not begin the ratification campaign until January 1898 at its state convention in Seattle. This late start handicapped the group's efforts from the outset.[144] WESA also failed to engage new supporters since its strategy was to team with already-existing groups—including prohibitionists such as the WCTU and ministers' associations—to promote ratification. The WCTU, for example, sent Olympia resident and activist Mary Page on a speaking tour around eastern Washington and Puget Sound to advocate for the amendment. Suffrage clubs were organized around the state.

M. L. PAGE
1878

M. E. PAGE
1878

They circulated petitions and conducted a partial house-to-house canvass of male voters. The petitions were ineffective because only women signed them. When the campaign only raised $500, WESA president Carrie Hill attributed the difficulty of fundraising to the distractions of the Spanish-American War and the Alaska gold rush. Lacking resources, suffragists aimed their efforts at the state's largest cities—Seattle, Tacoma, Olympia, and Spokane. By Hill's account, the campaigners distributed 5,000 copies of a thirty-page booklet containing testimonials from women voters in other states. She also noted that Henry Blackwell, editor of the *Woman's Journal*, sent 500 pieces of literature to each county in the state.[145]

Well-known suffragist Carrie Chapman Catt and her associate Mary G. Hay, both officers of the National American Woman Suffrage Association (NAWSA),[146] came to Washington in October 1898, just before the vote. Catt spoke in Seattle at the First Methodist Episcopal Church and at the Woman's Century Club, which she had helped start in 1891.[147] She also lectured in Tacoma, Ellensburg, and Spokane, and sent 62,000 pieces of literature to citizens of Washington State.[148]

Anti-suffrage forces worked actively against ratification. Brewing interests likely bankrolled New York anti-suffragist Mrs. W. Winslow Crannell, who established headquarters in Spokane and spoke about suffrage as a dangerous experiment that could damage womanhood. Spokane saloons warned of the results of women's votes and posted anti-suffrage placards in their windows.[149]

The amendment lost on November 8, 1898, by a vote of 30,540–20,658, which was a gain of 9,510 pro-suffrage votes over the 1889 tally. Carrie Hill fingered saloon interests for the loss; others blamed men's fears that if women gained the vote they would push through moral reforms like gambling control and rein in political bosses; still others pointed to the lack of firm Populist support for the measure.[150] The pairing of the Single Tax with suffrage on the same ballot may have influenced a negative vote. This radical measure, which lost by a wide margin, advocated taxing only land and exempting taxation of personal property and improvements.

The anti-suffrage vote was widespread and cut across demographic, ethnic, economic, and political lines. Even if Populists had actively supported the amendment, by 1898 they were losing steam as the state's economy rebounded from the depths of depression. Election day found few women at polling sites. Reflecting on the loss, the press said women were not interested in voting. The *Seattle Post-Intelligencer* said it appeared that women did not want full voting rights because they had not widely exercised their existing right to vote in school elections. *The Seattle Times* observed that when women wanted to vote they would achieve it and that it did not appear they really wanted it in this election.[151]

Despite the loss, supporters in 1898—Seattle's Western Central Labor Union of Seattle, Spokane's *Freemens Labor Journal*, and the Washington State Grange—became part of the coalition that would support the successful vote in 1910. Their 1898 experience would prove important; Hill stated that these "liberal and free-thought societies" were the hardest-working groups in support of the campaign.

The Twentieth-C

tury Campaign

After the 1898 defeat the Washington Equal Suffrage Association all but disbanded and maintained only nominal existence during the period around the turn of the twentieth century.[152] It took a national event in 1905, the NAWSA convention held in Portland, Oregon, as part of the Lewis & Clark Centennial Exposition, to rekindle the suffrage movement in Washington. After losses in California in 1896, Washington in 1898, and Oregon in 1900, suffragists hoped to launch a successful 1906 Oregon suffrage campaign using the centennial as a springboard. The enactment of initiative and referendum in Oregon in 1902 gave NAWSA leaders another avenue to pursue suffrage besides direct legislative action. Also, the growing popularity of Progressivism in Washington augured well for a resurgence of the suffrage movement in the Northwest. ★ The 1905 convention brought a number of seasoned suffrage pioneers to Portland to reinvigorate the region: Susan B. Anthony at age 85,

N. A. W. S. A.
June 28 to July 5, 1905

PORTLAND OREGON
"SACAJAWEA"

IN 1905 SUFFRAGE MOVEMENT LEADERS AT THE NATIONAL AMERICAN WOMAN SUFFRAGE ASSOCIATION CONVENTION SEIZED ON SACAGAWEA AS A SYMBOL FOR WESTERN WOMEN WHO WERE CAMPAIGNING FOR THE VOTE, CASTING HER AS AN EXAMPLE OF THE PARTNERSHIP BETWEEN WOMEN AND MEN IN SETTLING AND PROSPERING IN THE WEST.

Henry Blackwell, Antoinette Brown Blackwell—the first ordained woman minister in the United States and Henry Blackwell's sister-in-law—plus NAWSA president Anna Howard Shaw and, of course, Abigail Scott Duniway. Coinciding with the Lewis and Clark Exposition, the dedication of a statue of the Native American woman Sacagawea was a central event of the convention. Shaw and Anthony presided over the dedication in Portland's Washington Park. Indeed, Shaw invoked Sacagawea in her annual address to the NAWSA Convention: ★ *Sacajawea . . . your tribe is fast disappearing from the land of your fathers. May we, the daughters of an alien race who slew your people and usurped your country, learn the lessons of calm endurance, of patient persistence and unfaltering courage exemplified in your life, in our efforts to lead men through the pass of justice, which leads over the mountains of prejudice and conservatism, to the broad land of the perfect freedom of a true republic, in which men and women together shall in perfect equality solve the problems of a nation which knows no caste, no race, no sex in opportunity, in responsibility, or in justice! May "the eternal womanly" ever lead us on![153]*

★ Besides the allusion to the mythology of the "vanishing Indian," the dedicatory remarks served up an occasion for rhetoric about Sacagawea in terms of the suffrage movement.[154] Anthony said that this was "the first time in history that a statue has been erected in memory of a woman who accomplished patriotic deeds."[155] In any case, suffrage leaders seized

upon Sacajawea as a symbol to western women campaigning for the vote and cast her as an example of the partnership of women and men in settling and prospering in the West. ★ After the NAWSA convention had concluded, Ida Husted Harper, a writer and Anthony's protégé, and Antoinette Blackwell carried the enthusiasm for a revitalized movement on to Puget Sound where they met with several suffragists, including Fanny Leake Cummings, then president of the Washington Equal Suffrage Association.

FACING PAGE: "APOTHEOSIS OF SUFFRAGE." ALTHOUGH THIS 1896 DRAWING BY GEORGE YOST COFFIN WAS INTENDED TO SATIRIZE THE IDEA THAT SUSAN B. ANTHONY AND ELIZABETH CADY STANTON WERE GEORGE WASHINGTON'S EQUALS, MANY TODAY WOULD SAY THEIR EFFORTS ON BEHALF OF WOMEN'S RIGHTS MAKE THEM OUR MOST IMPORTANT "FOREMOTHERS."

ABOVE: NATIONAL AMERICAN WOMAN'S SUFFRAGE ASSOCIATION 1905 CONVENTION GATHERING. CENTER FRONT ARE, LEFT TO RIGHT, SUSAN B. ANTHONY, ABIGAIL SCOTT DUNIWAY, AND DR. ANNA HOWARD SHAW.

RIGHT: THE SMITH PREMIER NO. 2, C. 1900. WITH ITS CLASSIC DOUBLE KEYBOARD, IT WAS ONE OF THE MOST POPULAR TYPEWRITERS AROUND THE TURN OF THE 20TH CENTURY.

The New Woman

Women who became suffrage leaders in the twentieth century benefited from changes in the economic and social climate in Washington and across the nation. As new products and services became available to the middle class[156] and industrialization created demands for more women in the workforce at the turn of the twentieth century, women began to step out of traditional roles. They enrolled for higher education in record numbers, often going into the social services.[157] These women joined the ranks of the many other working-class and African American women who had long been in the workforce as domestics and factory workers, often using their expertise in social and settlement work to help their working-class sisters obtain better employment conditions.

The so-called "New Woman" also participated in clubs and extended her domestic concerns to "municipal housekeeping," demanding, for example, pure food and drug laws and better sanitation in cities. As the country became increasingly urbanized, households became consumers instead of solely producers of domestic goods. The rise of commercial culture influenced the media-oriented suffrage campaigns of the new century and became a backdrop to the resurgence of the women's suffrage movement and eventual success in Washington in 1910. Claiming that "the home does not stop at the street door," these municipal housekeepers came to realize that they needed the power of the vote to effect meaningful changes.[158]

One symbol of early-twentieth-century change for women was the bicycle. Anthony said it "did more to emancipate women than anything in the world." On bicycles women were able to get free of cumbersome clothing, go places on their own, and improve their physical fitness. Similarly, by the second decade of the twentieth century women were traveling in groups or alone in automobiles without male escort. Historian Virginia Scharff stated, "Climbing into an automobile, a woman rejected the cloister, certainly, and potentially also the female sphere of "hearth and home.""[159] Women suffragists used automobiles and car caravans for parades and campaigns, demonstrating their modern command of the vehicle as well as their "personal and political emancipation."[160] Groups displayed banners and

bunting on cars, which enabled campaigners to reach more voters, particularly in rural areas. During the suffrage campaign, Spokane activist May Arkwright Hutton owned and traveled in a luxurious Chalmers automobile. Washington suffragists used the "Blue Liner," a seven-passenger touring car, in 1910, and passed it on to California for their 1911 campaign.[161]

Women came to dominate the office workplace, where by 1910 they made up 83 percent of typists and stenographers.[162] This figure represented a significant increase from 1880 when 40 percent of these workers were female and 1900 when women made up 76.7 percent of office workers.[163] Historian Margery W. Davies found a number of reasons for the increase of female office workers by 1910, including the expanding economy and education of women. Women also worked more cheaply than men. Davies also noted that women were trained into clerical work as one of the few occupations requiring literacy for white, native-born women.[164]

These women were portrayed by the image of the "Gibson Girl," smartly dressed for work in an ensemble of a white shirtwaist and skirt. Although office work was preferable to factory and domestic employment, the work was still unglamorous, regimented,

and repetitive.[165] Large numbers of women also worked as telephone operators and department stores clerks, positions employers preferred to fill with educated, native-born, white females.[166] Alice Lord founded the Waitresses Union in Seattle in 1900 and joined with suffragists in the campaign for the right to vote. Seattle women sewed fabric onto the frames of airplane wings and drafted plans for new Boeing aircraft. As wage earners, they fueled labor's support for the vote and belied the notion that women were too frail for public life.

White middle-class women attended college and entered professions in increasing numbers and delayed marriage longer than had their counterparts a few decades earlier. Mary Leonard was the first woman admitted to the Washington Territorial Bar in 1884, and women increasingly joined such professions as social work, medicine, dentistry, and architecture.[167] Washington started three teacher training schools in the late 1800s—Cheney State Normal School in 1890, Washington State Normal School at Ellensburg in 1891, and State Normal School at New Whatcom (Bellingham) in 1899—all of which enrolled mostly women. Many educated and professional women became active suffragists in the 1909–1910 Washington campaign. The College Equal Suffrage League and other similar groups lent intellectual support to the cause.

Although backed by hundreds of less prominent women in the grassroots campaign, two individuals stand out as driving forces behind the 1909–1910 victory in Washington: May Arkwright Hutton and Emma Smith DeVoe. They embody Washington women's single-minded efforts to achieve the vote. Hutton and DeVoe did not always agree on tactics, but they used their individual political savvy to organize women east and west of the Cascades to convince Washington men to vote for equal rights.

FACING PAGE: PACIFIC TELEPHONE & TELEGRAPH COMPANY OPERATING ROOM IN SEATTLE, NOVEMBER 25, 1902.

THIS PAGE: CERTIFICATE QUALIFYING MARY LEONARD TO PRACTICE LAW IN WASHINGTON. IN 1884 SHE BECAME THE FIRST WOMEN ADMITTED TO THE WASHINGTON TERRITORY BAR.

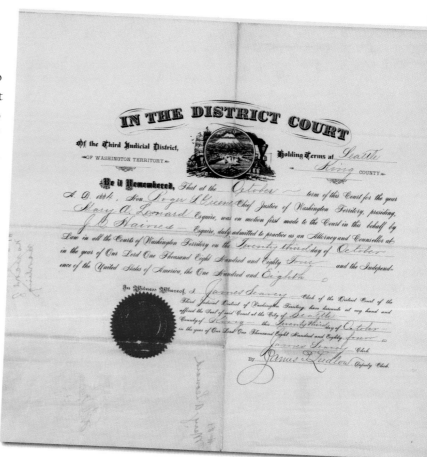

The Campaign Begins

As one of the national organizers sent to Oregon for the 1906 campaign, Emma Smith DeVoe worked from January to June of that year as a paid organizer under Anna Howard Shaw and NAWSA, organizing chapters of suffragists, setting up meetings, and giving lectures.[168] After her work in Oregon, DeVoe returned to Washington and reorganized WESA under the aegis of NAWSA. She began to mobilize local clubs, and by November 1906 had made important progress. NAWSA eventually paid DeVoe $100 per month, and her husband, who worked for the Northern Pacific Railroad, was able to provide her with a railroad pass.[169]

Aiding the state organization, Fannie Leake Cummings, Ellen S. Leckenby, and Max Wardall reincorporated WESA in April 1906. At the November 1906 convention WESA elected DeVoe as president—an office to which she was reelected in 1907, 1908, and 1909. Seattle activists Leckenby and Hester Miller organized speaking engagements for DeVoe throughout the state. The new suffrage clubs raised money, circulated petitions, wrote letters, and conducted debates. Their paid dues contributed to the salaries of the professional organizers.[170] These new clubs countered the assessment of the 1898 campaign failure that women did not want the right to vote.[171]

WESA headquarters was in Seattle's Arcade Building in an office shared with Dr. Cora Smith Eaton.[172] Originally from Illinois, Eaton had been active in North Dakota and Minnesota suffrage campaigns as well as holding offices in NAWSA. She came to the 1905 Portland NAWSA Convention and then set up her medical practice in Seattle in 1906. She became a pivotal figure and DeVoe's close associate during the Washington campaign.

From 1906 to 1908 suffrage leaders focused on organization, and from 1908 forward their emphasis was on campaigning. At the WESA State Convention in 1908 the executive committee authorized DeVoe to take charge of the effort to introduce women's suffrage legislation in the 1909 legislature that would amend the Washington constitution. According to historian T. Alfred Larson's account, there were by that time "75 clubs with more than 1,500 members [who] circulated petitions and obtained signatures of 10,000 men and women."[173] WESA delegates pledged $1,000 to finance the campaign.[174]

May Arkwright Hutton

May Arkwright was born in Ohio in 1860 and kept house for her father as a girl. An accomplished cook in maturity, May moved to Idaho in the 1880s after her first marriage failed. She was preparing meals in boarding houses near Coeur d'Alene when she met Levi "Al" Hutton, a railroad engineer, whom she married in 1887. Together they purchased a small interest in the Hercules Mine in the Coeur d'Alene Mountains, where May Hutton cooked for the miners and likely worked in the mine as well. In 1899 Al Hutton became embroiled in labor troubles endemic to that region. His wife was radicalized in this environment and remained a labor advocate the rest of her life. The Huttons' investment in the Hercules Mine paid off when they struck high-grade silver ore in 1901. May and Al prospered, and she turned her attention to charitable and political work. ☆ After women in Idaho gained the right to vote in 1896, May Hutton unsuccessfully ran for the Idaho legislature in 1904. The Huttons moved to Spokane in 1906, and May began to campaign for women's voting rights in Washington. At first aligned with DeVoe, whom she

had met during the Idaho campaign, Hutton assisted WESA in the 1909 Washington legislative victory. Hutton later split with DeVoe and formed the Washington Political Equality League during the 1909–1910 ratification campaign. In contrast to the ladylike DeVoe, Hutton had a distinctive, direct style and approach. She believed wholeheartedly in the power of the vote for working women and equality for women taxpayers. Her strategies and support appealed to important labor voters in eastern Washington. ☆ After the 1910 victory Hutton was one of the first women to serve on a Spokane jury. She also campaigned for the women's eight-hour workday. In 1912 she was one of the first female delegates to the Democratic National Convention. She continued her long-standing philanthropic work, especially with young women, and died in 1915 at the age of 55. Her husband continued the Huttons' charitable legacy, establishing the Hutton Settlement for children in 1919, which still endures today.[175]

The Legislative Strategy of 1909

The political climate favored the suffragists' efforts. By 1909 Republicans had lost their stranglehold on the legislature, providing an additional opportunity for support from a liberalizing Democratic Party and other Progressives in the legislature. The rise of the more urban oriented Progressive movement in Washington took hold as agrarian-centric Populism declined. Progressives advocated reforms like pure food legislation, regulation of alcohol and gambling, direct government by citizen initiative and recall, and corruption-free government. Progressives believed that "the rule of the majority should be expressed in a stronger government, one with a broader social and economic program and one more responsive to popular control."[176]

Women's suffrage complemented several Progressive reform goals and became identified with the march of reform in the West.[177] On the other hand, Progressivism did present some obstacles to women's suffrage. In the estimation of historian Marte Jo Sheeran, "Many of the progressives were middle class men, who believed that woman's place was in the home caring for her husband and children,

Emma Smith DeVoe

When Emma Smith was eight years old she attended a speech given by Susan B. Anthony on women's suffrage. When Anthony asked the crowd who favored women voting, Emma rose to her feet. Born in 1848 to an Illinois abolitionist family, she received an unusually good education for a young woman of this period and taught music at Eureka College in Illinois before marrying John DeVoe in 1880 and moving to Dakota Territory the following year. ✩ Supported by her husband, DeVoe's interest in politics and her membership in the WCTU naturally led her to advocate for women's rights. Anthony saw promise in her attractive appearance, singing voice, and talent as an organizer as well her "feminine," low-key political style. DeVoe worked as an organizer for NAWSA for years under the tutelage of Carrie Chapman Catt, traveling to many states, including North Dakota, Illinois, Iowa, and Kansas. In 1905 the DeVoes moved to Washington. Having taken a hiatus for several years, DeVoe returned to organizing in 1906, working for NAWSA first in Oregon and then in Washington. Despite having a reputation for an autocratic style of organizing, DeVoe's efforts were crucial to the success of the 1910 Washington campaign. ✩ After women won the vote in Washington, DeVoe founded the National Council of Women Voters (NCWV) in 1911 as a way of bringing voting women in western states together to agitate for a national women's suffrage amendment. She remained active in the NCWV and in 1919 approved a plan for it to merge with the League of Women Voters. Once the merger took place, she served on the first League of Women Voters council.[178] ✩ DeVoe managed to pressure Governor Louis Hart into calling a special legislative session for Washington to ratify the Nineteenth Amendment in 1920. She later became active in the Republican Party, which appointed her to a position on the Republican National Committee in the early 1920s. She thereafter contributed Republican commentary to the *Tacoma News Tribune* and died in 1927 at age 76. In recognition of her important role as an ardent advocate of women's rights, DeVoe was inducted into the National Women's Hall of Fame in Seneca Falls, New York, in 2000.[179]

suffragists who came from around the state to the capital to lobby their legislators.[183] These women, using persistent but low-key lobbying, are generally credited with the passage of the suffrage-enabling legislation in the house of representatives on January 29, 1909.

Carrie Hill, who had worked for the constitutional suffrage amendment in 1897, commented on the different tenor of the 1909 legislative session compared to previous years. She noted: "There has been no disposition on the part of legislators to regard the bill as a joke, as in former sessions, nor is the measure a football to be kicked around by the lawmakers. Instead every man we have approached has given Mrs. DeVoe and myself a respectful hearing, and many of the men have promised to work for the measure."[184] DeVoe, following the lead of Carrie Chapman Catt, and drawing upon her experience and characteristic demeanor, employed a "ladylike" but high-pressure strategy in the legislative session. Her principles for winning the vote included: "Keep the issue single. Be for nothing but suffrage; against nothing but anti-suffrage"; and "Always be good natured and cheerful."[185]

Suffragists argued effectively that they wanted the legislature to give the people (meaning male voters) of Washington a chance to decide on whether women should vote. The requirement for a statewide referendum to enact the amendment lifted the burden from legislators' shoulders to decide the issue themselves and served the ideals of direct democracy, which appealed to the Progressive ethos.

DeVoe drafted the suffrage legislation with Senator George Cotterill, a Seattle Democrat and reformer. Because it was a constitutional amendment, the legislation required a two-thirds majority for passage in both houses. The measure did not specify that it was a proposal for women's suffrage but simply stated that it was an amendment "relating to the qualifications of voters within this State." The amendment extended the right to vote to all women who otherwise met the qualifications for voting. This included the provisions that "Indians not taxed shall never be allowed the elective franchise" and that voters should be able to read and speak English. These

and not in the political arena championing causes or politicians."[180]

At the state suffrage campaign headquarters Adella Parker set up a publicity bureau composed of salaried men who provided information to every state newspaper. Activists presented individual legislators with large petitions signed by both men and women. This marked a substantial change from the 1898 campaign when activists submitted petitions to the entire legislature, an effort that proved ineffective. Spokane leader Hutton managed the petition drive while DeVoe took charge of laying the political groundwork for the 1909 legislative session.[181]

For its Olympia headquarters WESA rented a large house near the capitol. Hutton took up residence in her own suite of rooms at the Mitchell Hotel, also near the capitol building. The January 14, 1909, *Morning Olympian* reported that "the Washington Equal Suffrage Association... has secured apartments and the ballroom in the J. C. Horr residence. No hint that the legislators are to be beguiled with dances into voting for equal suffrage is given. The women in charge simply have secured the ballroom as a convenient gathering place."[182]

DeVoe spent the entire session in Olympia. She reportedly handpicked and trained the prominent elements already existed in the state constitution prior to the women's suffrage amendment.[186]

Representative T. J. Bell, a Tacoma Republican, introduced the bill in the house on January 20, 1909. After an initial referral it was reassigned to a committee more friendly to the cause—from the Constitutional Revision Committee to the Committee on Privileges and Elections—and was favorably reported back to the main body. The full house approved the measure with a narrow three-vote majority on January 29. Favorable passage relied on Progressive affiliation rather than party-line votes. The bill was not highly publicized in the press, receiving only passing mention. Racetrack gambling and local option prohibition received much more attention.[187] One exception was a series of cartoons drawn by an Olympia newspaper caricaturist, Teague Reynolds. He drew a series of panels characterizing the 1909 legislative campaign in Olympia that is classic in the catalog of suffrage imagery. The panels reflect the long history of using cartoons to skewer those involved in the civic arena, in this case creating caricatures of overbearing women and meek, henpecked men.

The legislative journey through the senate proved much more arduous. When the suffrage bill was introduced, Senator E. M. Williams of Seattle immediately moved to postpone the bill indefinitely. Cotterill rescued the situation by a motion to refer it to the Committee on Constitutional Revision. Concentrating these efforts, suffragists led by Seattle activist Leonia Brown organized a meeting in Williams's Seattle district and organized a petition in favor of the bill, but even these efforts did not sway him.

The final floor vote was postponed, precipitating a serious split between Hutton and DeVoe. Hutton wanted to press for immediate action before the end of the session, but DeVoe preferred to have a majority of legislators in favor of the bill before calling for a vote. Eaton insinuated that Hutton had talked about buying the votes of senators for $250 each and accused Hutton of using vulgar language in front of the legislators.[188] The senate eventually voted for the legislation on February 23, 1909, by a margin of 30–9, with three absent. By one account women in the galleries only fluttered handkerchiefs in celebra-

tion, reflecting the restrained tone of the campaign. Acting Governor Marion Hay[189] signed the bill on February 25, 1909, authorizing a statewide vote for ratification of the amendment in November 1910. At that time, statewide elections were held only in even-numbered years.

Legislators had various reasons for supporting the legislation. Seattle Senator George U. Piper was associated with the anti-prohibitionists, but he became a suffragist ally "in honor of his dead mother, who had been ardently in favor of women suffrage."[190] A perplexing part of the legislative dynamic was the absence of opposition by the saloon interests, which had been previously so effective in opposing woman's suffrage. Their posture may have been due to the preoccupation of the "wets" with the local prohibition bill option making its way through the legislature that session. DeVoe may also have co-opted saloon interests by enlisting Senator Piper and Representative Bell—both opposed to local prohibition—to advance the suffrage cause. A consistently reform-minded legislature perhaps determined that this group of persistent women deserved a chance to have the public decide on their right to vote.[191]

FACING PAGE: OLD CAPITOL IN OLYMPIA WHERE THE 1909 LEGISLATURE AUTHORIZED THE STATEWIDE VOTE TO AMEND THE WASHINGTON STATE CONSTITUTION FOR WOMEN'S SUFFRAGE.

THIS PAGE: SEATTLE LEGISLATOR GEORGE COTTERILL (1865–1958) DRAFTED THE 1909 SUFFRAGE AMENDMENT WITH EMMA SMITH DEVOE.

The 1909–1910 Ratification Campaign

*W*ashington women prepared to wage the same kind of womanly but effective campaign to ratify the amendment to the Washington State Constitution that had been successful in the legislature, including intensive lobbying. Suffrage groups had twenty months to work on swaying the male electorate before the public vote in November 1910.

This campaign phase had continued Progressive support. Some thought that enfranchised women would exclusively support Progressive causes, but DeVoe and other leaders were careful not to identify with specific reforms, such as prohibition. The suffragists' primary allies—the Grange, labor unions, and the Farmers Union—were also part of the Progressive movement. The support of these well-known groups helped legitimize the campaign.

The suffragists generally employed the "still hunt" strategy—using both one-on-one lobbying and working with key, influential groups of voters. The emphasis was not on rallies but on the personally intensive work of wives, mothers, and sisters to influence the men in their lives—the voters who would decide their fate. One campaign goal was for "each suffragist to as a matter of conscience win over before November 1910, ten voters not now committed to the amendment."[192] Women used the same rationale they had during the legislative process—the right to vote was a "matter of justice," not utilitarian. Women did not predict how they would vote on future ballot issues but advocated the franchise as way of attaining dignity and showing others that Washington men accorded women that dignity.

The campaign tailored its message to a wide variety of interests, reflecting the ideology that women and their roles were different in the West, paying homage to women pioneers.[193] *Votes for Women*, a newspaper first published in October 1909, was a major media initiative and the official organ of WESA. Missouri Hanna, an experienced newspaperwoman who also owned and edited the *Edmonds Review*, edited *Votes for Women* along with Seattle associate editors Adella M. Parker, Mary G. O'Meara, and Rose Glass. Hanna's daughters later joined the paper as staff members. The first issue of *Votes for Women* described "The Spirit of the West":

How Suffragettes Thanked Legislature

VOTES FOR WOMEN

On the name of the Wash.
Equal Suffrage Association
we thank you for voting to
submit our Bill to the voters
of the State at the next
general election.

Emma Smith DeVoe, Pres.
Ellen S. Leckenby, Sec'y

R 2, mch 16 - 1889

WOMAN SUFFRAGE PARTY

Controversy and Splintering in the Campaign

The campaign was not without dissension. The split between DeVoe and Hutton that had started during the 1909 legislative campaign widened. Splintering also came from other quarters, including professional and younger women who objected to DeVoe's autocratic demeanor. These schisms came to the fore at the 1909 NAWSA National Convention in Seattle, the first large event of the votes ratification campaign. Anticipating success in the 1909 legislature, DeVoe had invited NAWSA to hold its annual meeting in Seattle during the Alaska–Yukon–Pacific Exposition (AYPE) in July. Some delegates and officials traveled via a special Northern Pacific train, originating in Chicago on June 25, 1909, with eighty-five eastern suffragists aboard. Fanny Garrison Villard, wife of the Northern Pacific Railroad magnate Henry Villard and daughter of famed abolitionist William Lloyd Garrison, was part of the entourage, as were NAWSA president Anna Howard Shaw; treasurer Harriet Taylor Upton; author Charlotte Perkins Gilman; eastern women's rights advocate Henry Blackwell; and Frances Squire Potter, another NAWSA official.

After leaving Chicago, the train stopped in St. Paul, Minnesota, and then traveled on to Spokane where the local chamber of commerce feted the NAWSA leadership group—presenting them with buttons and badges and escorting them on a tour of the city. Hutton hosted the celebrated group of national suffrage leaders at a banquet at the Davenport Hotel's Hall of Doges in downtown Spokane.[196] Spokane Mayor N. S. Pratt welcomed the women to the city and presented a gavel to Shaw with which to open the convention in Seattle. It was made of wood from each of the four suffrage states bound together with a band of Idaho silver.[197]

The women of Washington want political equality with their brothers, not because they have been badly treated, but because they have been well treated. It is only those classes of people who have enjoyed rights and privileges who know how to appreciate them, and work for more. The laws in regard to women and children in Washington, are next best to those in the four equal suffrage states—probably because we did have equal suffrage here in territorial days. We want them second to none.[194]

Each issue of Votes for Women included a poster and often reflected the "western" flavor of the campaign with slogans such as: "Women Vote for President and All Other Officers in Wyoming, Utah, Idaho, and Colorado. Why not in Washington? Are the Women of Those States More Worthy or Are the Men of Those States More Just?" DeVoe stated that the suffrage impulse "came from the broad-shouldered, big-brained men of our great Northwest who made good their popular Western phrase 'A square deal for men must be accompanied by a square deal for women.'" Historian John Putnam noted that suffrage arguments made the connection between Washington women retaining community property rights—a primarily western phenomenon—and having a voice in their government.[195]

FACING PAGE: SEATTLE SUFFRAGISTS, C. 1909.

ABOVE, LEFT: NOTE FROM ONE OF EMMA SMITH DEVOE'S SCRAPBOOKS.

ABOVE, RIGHT: WOMAN SUFFRAGE PARTY SASH, C. 1900-1915, USED BY EDITH LEE HOLBROOK KEITH AND HER DAUGHTERS IN NEW YORK.

After leaving Spokane on June 29, the "Suffrage Special" made brief stops in Pasco, North Yakima, and Ellensburg so that suffragists could address crowds from the rear train platform. In Ellensburg 25 girls "passed through the train and distributed Kittitas strawberries and apples at the rear of the train. The train was showered with flowers."[198] The Suffrage Special's penultimate stop was in Tacoma, where the party toured Point Defiance before journeying on to Seattle for a reception at the Lincoln Hotel.

The NAWSA convention was held July 1–7, 1909, primarily in Seattle's Plymouth Congregational Church. WESA had met in a stormy session at the same location on June 30. The presidency of WESA became a topic of controversy as DeVoe sought to retain her title amidst Hutton's opposition. The Spokane suffragist had begun to resent DeVoe's heavy-handed management of the campaign and her paid position. Hutton saw a conflict between DeVoe's role as a paid organizer and the success of the campaign. She reasoned that DeVoe might have had a monetary reason to hope the campaign would fail. Hutton stated, "I do not consider those who make a profession of, and earn a livelihood in any reform, are the best elements for success."[199] Hutton, along with other prominent Seattle and Spokane advocates called "the insurgents," had met in April 1909 to come up with a plan for unseating DeVoe as president of WESA.[200]

Hutton recruited and likely paid for members for the Spokane Equal Suffrage Association to attend the WESA convention in Seattle. Cora Smith Eaton, who was chair of the credentials committee and treasurer of WESA, rejected the Spokane delegates. She made inflammatory statements about Hutton: "I believe you are ineligible to membership in the Washington Equal Suffrage Association because of your habitual use of profane and obscene language and of your record in Idaho as shown by pictures and other evidence placed in my hands by persons who are familiar with your former life and reputation."[201]

She promised not to make these allegations public unless Hutton pushed the credential issue for the clubs. Eaton also rejected twenty-two other clubs that were not loyal to DeVoe. The insurgents were not allowed to vote, and DeVoe won reelection as WESA president. NAWSA President Shaw was unhappy about the dissension in WESA and refused to seat DeVoe at the national convention. Instead, she seated two insurgents without voting rights—LaReine Baker of Spokane and Leonia Brown of Seattle. DeVoe lost her salary from NAWSA because she would not reconcile with the insurgents and afterward became permanently disaffected with Shaw.

The tumult of the 1909 conventions led to the creation of a multitude of new Washington suffrage organizations. Hutton established the Washington Political Equality League (WPEL) in July 1909. Carrie Hill and, later, Katherine Mackay, a wealthy former New York socialite, led the Equal Franchise Society (EFS), which was affiliated with the Seattle Suffrage

THIS PAGE: THE REVEREND DR. ANNA HOWARD SHAW (1847-1919) WAS PRESIDENT OF THE NATIONAL AMERICAN WOMAN SUFFRAGE ASSOCIATION WHEN THE GROUP HELD ITS 1909 CONVENTION IN SEATTLE.

FACING PAGE, TOP: *THE SEATTLE SUNDAY TIMES* FEATURED SOME OF THE LEADING NAWSA SUFFRAGISTS WHO ARRIVED IN SEATTLE VIA THE NORTHERN PACIFIC "SUFFRAGE SPECIAL" ON JUNE 29, 1909.

FACING PAGE, BOTTOM: DR. CORA SMITH EATON (LATER KING) (1867-1939) WAS A FOUNDING MEMBER OF THE MOUNTAINEERS, A PHYSICIAN, AND KEY ACTIVIST IN THE 1909-10 WASHINGTON SUFFRAGE CAMPAIGN.

Club.[202] DeVoe maintained control of WESA with the College Equal Suffrage League as a subsidiary. Adella Parker in Seattle and Sarah Commerford in Spokane headed college groups.

Although the mushrooming number of suffrage organizations might seem to have fragmented the efforts of the movement, historian John Putnam posited that "ideological inconsistency was one of the strengths of the campaign" since suffragists had to convince a diverse population of the merits of enfranchisement using arguments aimed at western men.[203] Indeed, using a novel tactic, Commerford, leading a group of 250 young women, announced in July 1909 that "each has taken a solemn vow to convert her suitor to woman's rights before entering upon an engagement."[204] Whether the women carried out this promise after the initial press coverage is unknown.

Katherine Smith, president of Seattle's Alki Point Suffrage Club, worked independently but cooperated with the Equal Franchise Society. Such clubs were joined by myriad local organizations throughout the state—most loosely affiliated with one or another group—that appealed to diverse interests. DeVoe, for example, enlisted the help of Finnish women, who had recently achieved the right to vote.[205] (Washington's 1910 population was nearly 16 percent Scandinavian.) She also worked through women's clubs, particularly those in eastern Washington, and the General Federation of Women's Clubs, which had become a powerful national organization. According to historian Karen J. Blair, women's clubs functioned as a training ground for suffragists.

Among the suffrage clubs noted in *Votes for Women* were the King County Political Equality Club, and chapters of various sizes in Ridgefield, Cherry Creek, Sunnyside, Kelso, Olalla, Walla Walla, Oakville, White Salmon, Mukilteo, Olympia, Alki Point, Puyallup, Chehalis, Hoquiam, Kelso, Mason County, Wilson Creek, Dayton, Waitsburg, Pomeroy, Asotin,

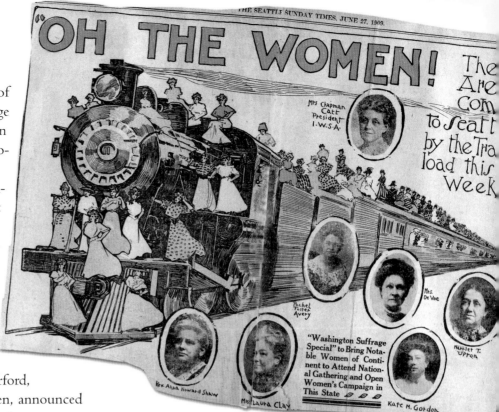

Clarkston, Prosser, Ellensburg, Prescott, Rainier Beach, Oakville, Dunlap, and Castle Rock. In Olympia women organized a Business Women's League for Equal Suffrage and an Olympia Equal Suffrage Club. There was a Young Woman's Education Club, Seattle Suffrage Club, Icelanders Club in Blaine, Tacoma South Side Equal Franchise Club, Scandinavian College Club, Aurora Suffrage Club, and a College of Puget Sound Equal Suffrage Club. In Everett suffragists contributed to local papers, supported an active publicity committee, and organized a canvassing group. They put a large yellow banner inscribed with "Vote for Amendment, Article VI, It Means: Votes for Women," downtown across Hewitt Avenue. Everett resident Ella Russell famously defended women's right to vote before a crowd of 6,500 during a Billy Sunday Crusade in Everett, rallying local support.[206]

The Alaska–Yukon–Pacific Exposition

$\mathcal{I}$n 1909 Seattle hosted the Alaska–Yukon–Pacific Exposition to celebrate its ties to Alaska and the Pacific Rim and to commemorate the Klondike Gold Rush. As the Lewis and Clark Centennial Exposition had done for Portland four years earlier, the AYPE was a chance for Seattle to show it had come of age as a major city. Because of the long, twenty-month campaign leading up to voter ratification of the suffrage amendment, the AYPE offered a major public relations opportunity. The event was actually delayed from 1907, the tenth anniversary of the gold rush, because the 300th anniversary of Jamestown, Virginia, took precedence that year.

Held on what is now the University of Washington campus, the exposition featured French Renaissance-style buildings as well as the more commercial "pay streak" with carnival attractions, rides, and exotic dancers. WESA hosted a permanent exhibit at the AYPE, sent a kite emblazoned with "Votes for Women" aloft, and distributed pins and leaflets. The AYPE included a "Women's Building," which still stands on the University of Washington campus, now named Cunningham Hall. The facility offered a lounge, childcare, a restaurant, and resting places for women at the fair as well as an impressive exhibit of Washington women's handcrafts and achievements.[207] The fair afforded the suffrage campaign an opportunity to appeal to other women's groups meeting in Seattle during the AYPE, including the Washington State Federation of Women's Clubs and the National Council of Women.

"Woman Suffrage Day" at the AYPE on July 7, 1909, was held in conjunction with the final day of the NAWSA convention. According to Alice Blackwell, every person entering the grounds received a "Votes for Women" ribbon. A kite and toy balloons emblazoned with the same slogan hovered over the fairgrounds.[208] The day opened with music and special events highlighted by remarks from famous speakers, including Blackwell, Harriet Upton, and Frances Potter. Idaho, Washington, and Utah women hosted receptions in the afternoon. WESA presided over a dinner at The Firs, fair headquarters of the Young Women's Christian Association (YWCA).[209] This final function (press accounts referred to it as a "love feast") was an opportunity for Washington suffragists to present a united front after the earlier infighting at the convention.[210]

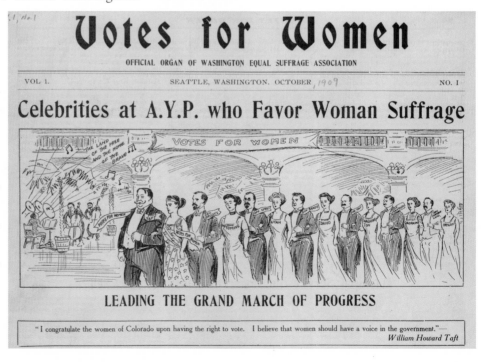

Votes for Women
OFFICIAL ORGAN OF WASHINGTON EQUAL SUFFRAGE ASSOCIATION

VOL. 1.   SEATTLE, WASHINGTON. OCTOBER, 1909   NO. 1

Celebrities at A.Y.P. who Favor Woman Suffrage

LEADING THE GRAND MARCH OF PROGRESS

"I congratulate the women of Colorado upon having the right to vote. I believe that women should have a voice in the government."—
William Howard Taft

Ministers, Organized Farmers, and Organized Labor

The sophisticated 1910 campaign cultivated the coalitions that had won the legislative victory—succinctly described as "ministers, organized farmers, and organized labor."[211] By one account, suffragists believed they could count 66,000 votes from farmers and labor alone as part of the progressive-farmer-labor coalition.[212]

Churches generally supported women's right to vote since they likely saw women voters as sharing a common interest in advocating for prohibition, but women also needed the support of churches to legitimize their campaign. Women preached from Seattle church pulpits on July 5, 1909, during the AYPE.[213] At the request of Emily Inez Denny, niece of Seattle pioneer and early suffrage promoter Arthur Denny, the Methodist Ministerial Association of Seattle came out for suffrage, as did the Danish Norwegian Church of Seattle. Many churches had observed DeVoe's request to preach a special pro-suffrage sermon in February 1910.

At the African-Methodist Conference in Seattle in August, DeVoe and Elizabeth Baker of Manette (now part of Bremerton) spoke and secured the conference's support for women's votes. At the event DeVoe talked about her abolitionist father and noted that his home was a station on the Underground Railroad. She noted how ironic it was that, just as African Americans had once asked her family for liberty, she was now asking them for the freedom of the vote.[214]

Two Seattle women compiled a leaflet in Scandinavian languages with sixteen Swedish and Norwegian ministers writing statements in favor of women's suffrage.[215] The Catholic Church did not endorse suffrage but individual priests proffered statements in favor of the amendment. In Spokane,

the Ministerial Association likewise passed resolutions of endorsement.[216]

Ministers were not unanimous in their support. Reverend Mark A. Matthews of Seattle's First Presbyterian Church was a very prominent "anti." In one of his sermons Matthews stated, "No sir! This country will never adopt female suffrage. If the ballot were extended to the women the star of America's glory would go down immediately, never to rise again."[217] The cover of the June 1910 *Votes for Women* featured a cartoon satirizing Matthews's opposition as an "old notion." Another opponent, Episcopal bishop William Croswell Doane, speaking to graduates of Saint Agnes School in Spokane in 1909, sounded the alarm. If women gained the right to vote, he worried, "your womanhood will gain nothing in its dignity and its true influence by the hysterical clamor which is employed in the pursuit of this chimera."[218]

Taking a page from previously successful campaigns in Colorado and Idaho, DeVoe established good relations with labor. She spoke at the state labor convention in 1908 and appointed Dr. Luema Greene Johnson as the campaign's superintendent of labor unions. Johnson was an active member of the Union Label League in Portland and Tacoma. Seattle labor leaders Blanche Mason, Grace Cotterill, and Alice Lord also supported the campaign.

Because of her storied experience in the northern Idaho labor conflicts, Hutton likewise identified closely with labor and appealed to working men in eastern Washington. After their split with DeVoe in July 1909, Hutton and LaReine Baker set up what

FACING PAGE: THE ALASKA-YUKON-PACIFIC EXPOSITION TOOK PLACE FROM JUNE 1 TO OCTOBER 16, 1909, ON LAND THAT LATER BECAME THE UNIVERSITY OF WASHINGTON CAMPUS. IN TERMS OF MARKETING, THE FAIR SERVED AS AN IMPORTANT JUMPING OFF POINT FOR THE SUFFRAGE CAMPAIGN.

THIS PAGE: THIS CARTOON FROM THE MAY 1910 ISSUE OF *VOTES FOR WOMEN* MAKES REFERENCE TO THE REVEREND MARK MATTHEWS'S OPPOSITION TO WOMEN'S SUFFRAGE.

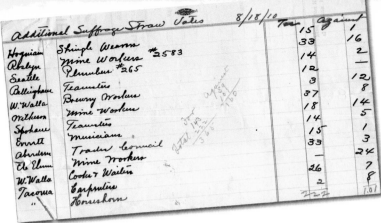

they called "Camp Equality" at Liberty Lake near Spokane to organize the Washington Political Equality League (WPEL) as a separate organization from WESA and to train suffragists from around the state.[219] The WPEL appointed labor precinct captains and liaisons in Spokane. Mrs. Harry (Maude) Jarvis, wife of the president of the Spokane's Central Labor Council; Julia Wilson, a longtime Spokane laundress who was fondly called "Mother" by the 700 women laundry workers in the city; and Sadie Coates, wife of Spokane socialist labor official David Coates and secretary of the Equal Suffrage Association of Spokane, spoke out for the movement. Rose Bassett Moore (Ascherman), Spokane Union Label League and Trades Council organizer, also worked in eastern Washington.[220] According to one account, Hutton guaranteed funds for speakers addressing labor groups; labor unions also raised funds for campaigners.[221]

At its 1910 convention, the State Federation of Labor unanimously adopted a resolution favoring women's suffrage and its president, Charles R. Case, urged the local unions to "put forth their most strenuous efforts to carry the suffrage amendment... and make it the prominent feature of their work during the coming months."[222] Labor unions favored suffrage because they saw women voters as favoring progressive, labor-friendly legislation, notably the eight-hour day for women. Labor-friendly women would also add to the unions' strength at the ballot box. The Washington State Federation of Labor conducted a straw vote in August 1910 in which only nine of forty-two locals opposed suf-

ABOVE: SOME OF THE RESULTS FROM THE AUGUST 1910 STRAW VOTE CONDUCTED BY THE STATE FEDERATION OF LABOR.

RIGHT: LIBBIE LORD (1850-1915) OF OLYMPIA WAS THE GRANGE TRUSTEE FOR THE WASHINGTON EQUAL SUFFRAGE ASSOCIATION AND REPRESENTED THE GRANGE AT NATIONAL SUFFRAGE CONVENTIONS.

frage. Among those opposed were the brewery workers of Walla Walla; farriers of Tacoma; lathers of Spokane, typographers of Walla Walla; bartenders, cooks, and waiters of Cle Elum; brewery workers of Seattle; typographers of Olympia; and bartenders of Raymond—generally reflecting the concern of the "wets" that women would vote for prohibition.

Suffragists also drew on significant support from the Washington State Grange and the Farmers Union. From its earliest inception in Washington in 1889, the Grange was an equal rights organization with women serving in important roles. Grangers promoted women's suffrage tirelessly through their newspaper *Pacific Grange Bulletin* and in other venues. Even prior to the 1909–1910 campaign, WESA and the Grange had joined in 1906 to promote a legislative resolution to

keep saloons and pool halls at least five miles away from Washington State College in Pullman—the land-grant university many rural students attended.[223]

In addition to general support, Olympia and Thurston County suffragists Lena Meyer, Clara Lord, and Libbie Lord spearheaded the effort to secure a straw ballot at the State Grange Convention in 1910. Some 13,000 members of the state Grange voted five to one for women's right to vote in their September straw poll—foreshadowing victory in November 1910.

In 1907 Washington's first Farmers Union local had organized in Waitsburg, and the Washington State Union was created in Pullman in 1908. The Farmers Union advocated for farmers on issues related to agriculture and created cooperatives to purchase goods and to market and store crops.[224] The farmers organized to compete with other workers' unions and supported reforms like initiative, recall, referendum, parcel-post delivery, and other Progressive issues. Like the Grange, the Farmer's Union endorsed the suffrage amendment at its state convention in 1910.[225]

The "Womanly Approach"

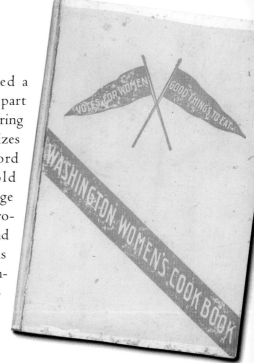

eVoe, Hutton, and other Washington suffragists generally conducted a "womanly" campaign. The *Washington Women's Cook Book* was one of the campaign's primary fundraising projects. Linda Deziah Jennings, a suffragist activist from La Conner, edited the cookbook. According to her family, Jennings was ill and could only work from her home on the project. DeVoe noted that the cookbook had two purposes: "One was, of course, the money and the other was the vindication of the slur put upon suffragists that they have no domestic traits."[226] *Collier's* quoted her as saying that "the book has made us friends among the men."[227] The volume is also notable as women shared their treasured family recipes for the cause they believed in. Contributors included Jennings's sisters and mother, and many other suffragists. It sold for one dollar and featured regular cookbook sections peppered with pithy quotes about women's rights and legal arguments supporting women's suffrage. Adella Parker penned a special article recounting the suffrage saga of the 1880s: "How Washington Women Lost the Ballot." Other distinctive sections of the publication included "Sailors Recipes," a "Mountaineers' Chapter," a "Vegetarian Department," and sections on housewifery and beauty secrets. Three thousand copies were printed, and Jennings fronted the cost of the publication of the cookbooks with a $100 loan.

By July 1910 the printing bill was paid and WESA gave 100 copies to each of the other states with a suffrage amendment pending in 1910—Oregon, South Dakota, and Oklahoma.

Building on the idea of suffragists as housewives, the *Tacoma News Tribune* featured a "Kitchen Contest" as part of the campaign, offering seventy dollars in prizes for the best 250-word essays on household management. Suffrage clubs also offered programs on pure food and provided model menus to assure men that dinner would continue to appear on the table even if women won the vote.[228]

A Modern Media Campaign

he media campaign adopted modern tactics that previously had been considered as "male." These included publishing a newspaper and writing newspaper editorials and news items; displaying banners, posters, or floats; and participating in other publicity-rich opportunities. Cora Smith Eaton went so far as to say that, "scientific advertising placed the fifth star upon the woman's suffrage flag and gave citizenship to 175,000 women."[229]

Votes for Women, the suffrage newspaper first published in October 1909, was a major media initiative and the official organ of WESA. The first issue made clear the paper's goals:

> VOTES FOR WOMEN *asks the attention of the public to the general question of woman's political enfranchisement and to the special consideration of the amendment granting suffrage to women which is to be voted on in this state in November, 1910. It will give the news of the progress of the suffrage campaign in*

ABOVE: THE *WASHINGTON WOMEN'S COOK BOOK* FEATURED RECIPES AND ARGUMENTS FOR WOMEN'S SUFFRAGE.

LEFT: LA CONNER SUFFRAGIST LINDA DEZIAH JENNINGS EDITED THE COOKBOOK AND FRONTED THE COST OF THE PUBLICATION WITH A $100 LOAN. BY JULY 1910 THE PRINTING BILL WAS PAID AND WESA GAVE 100 COPIES TO EACH OF THE THREE STATES THAT HAD A SUFFRAGE AMENDMENT PENDING IN 1910—OREGON, SOUTH DAKOTA, AND OKLAHOMA.

Washington and also items of interest with reference to the struggle being made through the word to secure woman her political rights. The magazine will be issued monthly and will be the official organ of the Washington Equal Suffrage Association. [230]

The paper listed donations from individuals and groups as well as events like the AYPE and Women's Days at the Puyallup Fair in 1909 and 1910. Along with biographical vignettes of suffragists, the paper provided a general history of the suffrage movement,

UPPER RIGHT: BRITISH WOMEN'S FREEDOM LEAGUE PIN.

ABOVE: POSTER BRIGADES, OFTEN ORGANIZED BY THE COLLEGE EQUAL SUFFRAGE LEAGUE, OPERATED IN MANY COMMUNITIES.

FACING PAGE, TOP: THE GRANGE, LABOR, AND FARMERS UNION ESCORT WOMEN TO THE BALLOT BOX IN THIS IMAGE FROM THE AUGUST-SEPTEMBER 1910 ISSUE OF *VOTES FOR WOMEN*.

FACING PAGE, BOTTOM: CHANGING ROLES FOR WOMEN WERE PART OF THE EARLY-TWENTIETH-CENTURY SOCIAL DEBATE. *TACOMA TRIBUNE*, JUNE 22, 1913.

included the texts of pro-suffrage addresses given around the state and nation, and excerpted other newspaper accounts related to suffrage. Most important, the paper detailed the myriad statewide efforts for the suffrage campaign, reinforcing its grassroots nature and presenting an important portrait of the strategies and rationales these ardent women used.

Each issue included a poster for subscribers to hang, featuring various pithy slogans such as: "Lincoln Said Women Should Vote"; "Give Women the Ballot for the Sake of the Children"; "Mark Twain Says: 'I would like to see the ballot in the hands of Every Woman.'" The paper even printed a recipe for poster paste. Poster brigades statewide ensured that broadsides found their way to communities large and small.[231] Seattle activist Edith DeLong Jarmuth wrote another widely distributed poster entitled "Why Washington Women Want the Ballot," noting eight specific reasons headed by "because those who obey laws should have something to say as to their making." In all, Washington women distributed over a million campaign pieces.[232]

Votes for Women published questions and answers about how women voted in other suffrage states and sought to answer queries such as whether or not "objectionable" women voted in those states and if voting affected divorce rates. To further lend credibility to the movement, the newspaper also included a "Roll of Honor" of recognizable figures who supported women's right to vote—"Preachers, Men of Letters, and Educators for Suffrage"—and similarly listed "Distinguished Women Who Have Declared Themselves for Women Suffrage."

Local newspapers were important suffrage organs as well. "Press workers" supplied news items to local newspapers in a number of counties.[233] By 1910 Minnie J. Reynolds, an experienced writer recruited from Colorado, was providing two daily suffrage columns to the Spokane *Spokesman-Review*. The *Seattle Star* conducted a poll among its female readers to see if they wanted the vote.[234] Alki Suffrage Club president Katherine Smith edited a daily column of suffrage news in the *Star*.

A new publication in 1910, the *Seattle Mail*, also editorialized for suffrage. Sam A. Perkins, who published eleven newspapers in Washington, ordered his editors to support suffrage.[235] Many newspapers around the state editorialized for woman's suffrage and aided the cause by publishing accounts of the militant tactics of English suffragettes and contrasting them to Washington women's moderate approach.[236] Henry Blackwell sent nearly four hundred copies of his paper, the *Woman's Journal*, to the state and promised to continue doing so until the November 1910 amendment vote, saying, "This I consider to be my dear wife, Lucy Stone's, contribution to the cause which she loved more dearly than life itself."[237]

Other Strategies

dherents conducted poll list canvasses, which Carrie Chapman Catt had used effectively in the 1896 Idaho campaign. Although in Idaho men canvassed the precincts, in Washington both men and women performed the arduous task. In the canvass, volunteers copied the poll lists in all counties of the state, noting the name, nationality, occupation, and address of all individual voters, and then sent the lists to WESA campaign headquarters where workers divided the lists by ward and precinct.

They asked each voter, "Will you vote for woman's suffrage in November 1910?" and noted objections if the man was opposed.

The goal was to complete the canvassing by June 1910 in order to have speakers and other resources allocated to areas where they were most needed. From *Votes for Women* accounts, it is likely only Thurston and Kitsap counties completed the canvass, although Pierce, Island, King, Yakima, Kittitas, Lewis, Clark, Mason, and Walla Walla counties were at least partially completed— about 50,000 names were gathered statewide. Grange members helped with this task, and the Kelso Suffrage Club paid for the blank poll list forms.[238]

Adopting another of the strategies crafted for the 1896 Idaho campaign, WESA created an advisory committee of representatives from other enfranchised states to assure Washingtonians that suffrage was a workable change. Governors James H. Brady of Idaho, John F. Shafroth of Colorado, Benton Brooks of Wyoming, and William Spry of Utah, along with Carrie Chapman Catt and Judge Ben Lindsey of Colorado, spoke on behalf of the campaign. The July 1910 issue of *Votes for Women* featured an article entitled "How Woman Suffrage Works in Idaho," by Idaho senator William E. Borah. Former Colorado governor Albert W. McIntire praised women voters in the paper.

Organizers generally discouraged national speakers from campaigning in-state, reflecting the philosophy that Washington women knew the men of their jurisdiction better than national organizers and could devise strategies and arguments that would best appeal to them. However, many nationally known activists worked on behalf of the Washington suffrage effort. The 1909 NAWSA Convention in Seattle featured major suffragists of the era, including Anna Howard Shaw, Charlotte Perkins Gilman, and Rachel Foster Avery. Senior statesman for the cause, Henry Blackwell, also spoke before the convention as a return campaigner. Before his death on September 7, 1909, Blackwell donated $100 to the Washington campaign. Longtime Oregon suffragist Abigail Scott Duniway and *The Woman's Tribune* editor Clara Bewick Colby campaigned in Washington. Minnie Reynolds recruited Montanan Jeannette Rankin to join the Washington campaign. Rankin had worked briefly as a social worker in a Spokane children's home and later attended the University of Washington in Seattle. Rankin's participation in Washington was her first public role in a career that would span decades.[239] She also campaigned successfully for women's suffrage in Montana in 1914 and in 1916 became the first woman elected to Congress.[240]

The WCTU had a long and varied relationship with the suffrage movement. Some leaders, particularly Abigail Scott Duniway, blamed prohibition advocates for the losses in both Washington and Oregon in the nineteenth and early twentieth centuries. In 1910 WCTU officers supported the campaign while the rank and file organized institutes, parlor meetings, and public addresses, and distributed leaflets.[241] The WCTU posted billboards that read: "Give the Women a Square Deal. Vote for the Amendment to Art. VI." Generally, however, the WCTU kept a low profile as part of the "still hunt" strategy of the campaign and followed what proved to be a successful approach during the

LEFT: THE WHITE RIBBON WAS A WCTU SYMBOL FOR PURITY.

ABOVE: THE LOYAL TEMPERANCE LEGION (LTL) WAS A CHILDREN'S ORGANIZATION OF THE WCTU. THE RIBBON SHOWS THE FIRST SLOGAN OF THE LTL AIMED AT YOUNG BOYS.

FACING PAGE, UPPER RIGHT: EQUAL REPRESENTATION—ESPECIALLY FOR TAXPAYERS—WAS A POTENT ARGUMENT DURING THE SUFFRAGE CAMPAIGN.

FACING PAGE, CENTER: CARRIE CHAPMAN CATT (1859-1947), WHO LIVED IN SEATTLE IN THE EARLY 1890S, DONATED $500 TO THE WASHINGTON CAMPAIGN. SHE WAS PRESIDENT OF THE INTERNATIONAL WOMAN SUFFRAGE ALLIANCE AT THE TIME, AND LATER HEADED NAWSA.

legislative session—not antagonizing the "wets." Cora Smith Eaton explained how the strategy was accomplished: "In a private conference called early in the campaign . . . an agreement was reached that, in order not to antagonize the "whiskey" vote, the temperance women would submerge their hard-earned honors and let the work of their unions go unheralded. They kept the faith."[242]

After kicking off the campaign at the AYPE in Seattle, suffragists continued to use fairs and chautauquas—traveling educational gatherings—to spread the word about women's right to vote. Several fairs featured a "Woman's Day," including the Puyallup Fair in 1909 and 1910, and the 1910 North Yakima State Fair, Walla Walla County Fair, Snohomish County Fair, and Touchet Valley Fair in Dayton. Suffragists entered a decorated automobile in the 1910 Spokane Interstate Fair parade and the WPEL published a daily paper during the event. Women made appeals at the chautauqua on Whidbey Island in July 1910 and at a Bellingham event. Hutton reportedly put "Votes for Women" banners on the elephants in a Ringling Brothers circus parade in Spokane during the campaign.[243]

Female organizers used male operatives to travel and talk to men on trains and boats, as well as in hotel lobbies and lumber camps about suffrage and engaged "a good politician" to work the waterfront (presumably Seattle).[244] Speakers went to the State Old Soldier's Home at Annapolis (near Port Orchard), Women's Christian Temperance Union meetings, and Good Templars (a men's temperance group) gatherings. Female organizers played to men's ideas about proper gender roles, too, to elicit male support for female suffrage. Instead of speaking at a Grand Army of the Republic (Civil War veterans) encampment, for example, Hutton baked and served eighty of her famous cherry pies, say-

ing, "Boys, I'm no speechmaker—I'm only a cook," securing along the way men's promises to vote for suffrage and "to compel all their comrades to do the same."[245]

Working through the WPEL, Hutton tailored the campaign approach in eastern Washington to appeal to the specific interests of social and economic groups residing there. Minnie Reynolds, an experienced Colorado writer and campaigner, spoke in Spokane in August and September 1910. The Colorado Equal Suffrage Association, of which Reynolds was a member, initially donated $100 for her work. Hutton later hired her outright to pen a weekly column in the Spokesman-Review.[246]

The WPEL's 1910 Labor Day Parade float in Spokane was the most flamboyant of the organization's activities, designed to stir the emotions of middle- and upper-class women—and the men who would enfranchise them—by equating non-voting women with the less desirables in society who were also without the elective franchise. At its four corners the elaborate float featured a mother with children at her knee, a nurse in uniform with a red cross, a business woman, and salesgirl behind a counter. Hutton sat in the center of the float with a stack of paper (representing her status as a major taxpayer). Iron cages stood at both ends of the float—one holding a convict in stripes, the other holding an "idiot." Chains ran from the waists of each of these unfortunates to every woman on the float. Banners proclaimed "Idiots, Criminals, and Women Cannot Vote."[247]

Although decidedly unpleasant, this kind of imagery was used by suffragists in the years before 1910 to emphasize their inferior status. One of the most famous images in that tradition is "American Woman and Her Peers," created in the 1890s. The drawing showed reformer and Women's Christian Temperance Union president Frances E. Willard with a Native American man, a convict, a mentally disabled man, and a madman—all of whom could not vote. The designer, Henrietta Briggs-Wall, said of the image, "It strikes the women every time. They do not realize that we are classed with idiots, criminals, and the insane as they do when they see that picture. Shocking? Well, it takes a shock

Women Mountaineers

Whether women possessed the physical and mental strength to participate in strenuous outdoor activities was an ongoing debate in the suffrage movement. Through their exploits, women mountaineers definitively answered that question. In July 1909 Dr. Cora Smith Eaton and several other women joined the Seattle-based Mountaineers Club (Eaton was a founding member) and participated in a climb to the summit of Mount Rainier as an adjunct event of the Alaska–Yukon–Pacific Exposition. Eaton planted the AYPE flag, which included the "Votes for Women" slogan, at the summit.[248] ☆ An active climber, Eaton was the first woman to reach the East Peak of Mount Olympus on August 15, 1907, in what is now Olympic National Park.[249] She went on to summit all six major peaks in Washington. Eaton was not the only suffragist climber. The Kangley sisters—Louise, Helen, Lucy, and Gertrude—who were active Seattle suffragists, attempted to climb Mount Rainier in August 1908, but bad weather forced them to unfurl their "Votes for Women" banner near Gibraltar Rock below the summit.[250] Spokane suffragist and socialite LaReine Baker ascended Pike's Peak in Colorado in late 1909, likewise planting a "Votes for Women" banner. She was probably campaigning for Washington since Colorado women had gained the right to vote in 1893.[251] These active, strong, adventurous leaders personified the "New Woman" of the suffrage movement in 1909–1910.

The Mountaineers on their annual outing in 1909 at the summit of Mount Rainier. Dr. Cora Smith Eaton attached a "Votes for Women" banner to the Alaska-Yukon-Pacific Expostion flag placed at the summit during the climb.

(Copyright 1911 by Henrietta Briggs-Wall.)
AMERICAN WOMAN AND HER POLITICAL PEERS.
In many states women are classed, politically, with idiots, convicts, the insane, and Indians—**not allowed to vote.** Women do not, however, escape taxation.
"Taxation without representation is tyranny."
"Resistance to tyranny is obedience to God."

to arouse some people to a sense of injustice and degradation."[252]

The WPEL and Hutton agreed with WESA relative to feminist militancy. Hutton reportedly waved off English suffragette Emmeline Pankhurst from visiting the state in the fall of 1909. Hutton was quoted in the *Spokesman-Review* as saying, "I note with satisfaction that our state is not be afflicted with a visitation from Mrs. Pankhurst. . . . The state of Washington does not need that kind of persuasion to induce the voters to perform the simple act of justice of according women political equality."[253] Hutton confirmed that both DeVoe and Carrie Hill of the Washington Equal Franchise Society agreed with her decision to avoid using militant suffragette tactics in the state. Hutton, however, did believe in "an aggressive field campaign," as long as women retained their "womanliness and dignity."[254] Using this strategy, WPEL members participated in parades, toured in decorated cars, and demonstrated at city council meetings.

ABOVE: "AMERICAN WOMAN AND HER POLITICAL PEERS," DESIGNED BY HENRIETTA BRIGGS-WALL OF KANSAS, PLACES FRANCES C. WILLARD (CENTER), WCTU PRESIDENT FROM 1879 TO 1898, IN COMPANY WITH "UNDESIRABLE" CLASSES OF MEN WHO ALSO DID NOT HAVE VOTING RIGHTS.

RIGHT: SINCE THE WORDING ON THE 1910 BALLOT DID NOT SPECIFICALLY INCLUDE THE WORDS "WOMAN SUFFRAGE," THESE FLYERS HELPED VOTERS UNDERSTAND THE BALLOT TITLE, "QUALIFICATIONS OF VOTERS."

Campaign Hurdles

Given the history of resistance to suffrage activities, surprisingly little organized opposition surfaced during the campaign. Writings about the campaign often state that the pro-suffrage strength was never evident to the opposition. Seattleite Eliza Ferry Leary, daughter of Washington's first governor and "among the highest taxpayers in the State" was the representative of the National Association Opposed to Woman Suffrage. She accepted the office, but then did nothing.[255] Eaton noted that the campaign "was remarkable for the fact that our so-called enemies served in an auxiliary capacity as friends and helpers."[256] Surprisingly, the "wets" did not actively campaign against the amendment as they had done in 1898. Mrs. Frances Bailey, an anti-suffragist from Portland, Oregon, spoke in some western Washington locations.[257] Historian Marte Jo Sheeran observed that suffrage was not a high-profile issue during the election, as evidenced by the press accounts of the time.[258] The anti-suffrage contingency that was typically most vocal—the wets—were busy fighting local-option prohibition battles in 1910. They may have assumed Washington's suffrage amendment would fail as had suffrage votes in Oregon in 1906 and 1908 and in Washington in 1898.

The 1910 ratification campaign cost $17,000, with the largest single contribution of $500 coming from Carrie Chapman Catt, a former Washingtonian who was then serving as president of the International Woman Suffrage Association.[259] Other national contributors included New York suffrage groups and the Massachusetts Suffrage Association, which donated $100 and paid the expenses of Alfred Brown, a suffrage speaker who traveled to Washington. Major organizational contributors, labor unions, and the Grange combined donated $1,000.[260] Mostly, however,

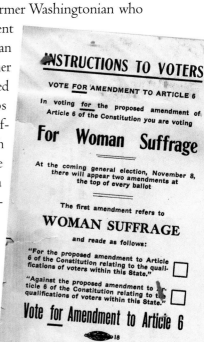

INSTRUCTIONS TO VOTERS

VOTE FOR AMENDMENT TO ARTICLE 6

In voting for the proposed amendment of Article 6 of the Constitution you are voting

For Woman Suffrage

At the coming general election, November 8, there will appear two amendments at the top of every ballot

The first amendment refers to

WOMAN SUFFRAGE

and reads as follows:

"For the proposed amendment to Article 6 of the Constitution relating to the qualifications of voters within this State." ☐

"Against the proposed amendment to Article 6 of the Constitution relating to the qualifications of voters within this State." ☐

Vote for Amendment to Article 6

18

the money came from small contributors. Eaton noted that money came from "cake sales, apron showers, sewing bees, and nickels and dimes saved out of the grocery and millinery bills of a thousand women."[261] Fundraising events ran the gamut from dancing and chocolate parties, food sales, fortune-telling, card parties, and coffee klatches to "Chinese parties," a "Political Equality Whist Club," a "Mountaineer's Campfire," and "Dutch treat luncheons." Even productions of George Bernard Shaw's play, *How She Lied to Her Husband*, became suffrage fundraisers. WESA expended about $8,000 on the campaign; WPEL, $3,500; and the Equal Franchise Society, $1,500.

Campaigners paid close attention to the wording and position of the ballot title in 1910, since many believed inattention to the title contributed to the earlier failures of women's suffrage votes. In 1889 both prohibition and suffrage were on the same ballot, and in 1898 women's suffrage was paired with the "single-tax" referendum—both controversial topics. Suffrage was one of two amendments to the Washington State Constitution on the 1910 ballot. The second issue was a non-controversial amendment providing for a mid-term gubernatorial election when a vacancy occurred. The word *suffrage* was not in the ballot title. The choices read: "FOR the proposed amendment to Article 6 of the constitution relating to the qualifications of voters within the state" and "AGAINST the proposed amendment." Both those for and against the suffrage amendment distributed printed slips with instructions for voters. "Vote for the Amendments," was an even simpler pro-suffrage tactic that did not distinguish between the two ballot measures.[262] According to the *History of Woman Suffrage* account of the campaign, Senator William H. Paulhamus of Puyallup gave the campaign advance information as to the exact wording and position of the amendment at the top of the ballot.[263] This allowed the campaign to simplify the ballot instructions, explaining that voters should "Vote for Amendment to Article VI at the Top of the Ballot." Suffragists mounted seven-by-ten-foot banners at strategic locations with that wording.[264]

The Election

After twenty months of organizing, canvassing, and campaigning, suffragists continued their sophisticated political strategy right up to election day. The August–September 1910 issue of *Votes for Women* gave nine items for adherents to follow to ensure a November victory:

1. Ask your friends to vote for the amendment. Ask every voter.
2. Ask the business people with whom you deal to help you get the ballot.
3. "Wear a "Votes for Women" pin. THIS IS MOST IMPORTANT. It will bring the amendment many a vote and besides it often opens a way to present the subject."
4. Send Votes for Women to your friends and to strangers.
5. Help with the poll list canvass.
6. Distribute suffrage literature (leave in steamers and on street cars).
7. Put up a suffrage poster (even a timid woman can do this).
8. Help in the press work.
9. Let people know you are alive in this campaign and the cause is won.

Confident after several positive editorials in major newspapers throughout the state, campaigners were out in force on rainy November 8, 1910. Organizers stationed two women and one man at each polling place. The women handed out cards asking for the vote on the first amendment while the male observer watched the vote tabulation. From earlier failures suffragists had learned hard lessons about guarding the integrity of the voting process, particularly with the ballot irregularities in 1889.[265]

The vote result was 52,299–29,676 in favor of ratification of the women's suffrage amendment—a margin of nearly two to one.[266] Every county voted in favor of the amendment, with greater pluralities in Puget Sound counties than in eastern Washington. Support cut across party lines as well as racial and ethnic, urban and rural populations; and there was little statistical difference between foreign- versus native-born, or educated versus uneducated voters. Surprisingly, no statistical difference existed between wets and dries on the suffrage issue or between reformers and non-reformers.[267] Washington joined the four western states where women had already won the vote—Wyoming (1890), Colorado (1893), Utah (1896), and Idaho (1896). Washington women and suffragists nationwide celebrated Thanksgiving Day on November 24, 1910, in gratitude for Washington women's victory and in celebration of the addition of a fifth star to the national suffrage flag. Governor Hay officially signed the proclamation of adoption on November 28, 1910. Twenty-two years had passed since the Territorial Supreme Court had last taken away Washington women's right to vote.[268]

The stunningly decisive victory in 1910 is widely credited with reinvigorating the national movement. When Washington joined her western sisters in 1910, it had been fourteen years since a state had enacted irrevocable women's suffrage. Male voters in Oregon, South Dakota, and Oklahoma all failed to enfranchise women in 1910. Washington's suffrage victory can be considered a "dam-breaker"; amendments giving women the right to vote quickly followed in several other states—California in 1911; Oregon, Kansas, and Arizona in 1912; Alaska Territory in 1913; and Montana and Nevada in 1914.

Newspapers generally downplayed the role women played in achieving victory. For example, the *Seattle Post-Intelligencer* headlined the results with "Women of the State Get the Ballot by Gift of Men."[269] In a post-victory summation, May Hutton gave liberal credit to the male voters who voted for suffrage in Washington, "I attribute the success of the movement largely to the broad-minded ideas of the men of Washington, who stand for a square deal in all things." Likewise, DeVoe thanked the men of Washington, "who by their vote gave their mothers, wives, and sisters equal franchise."[270] Despite this humility, women's tireless efforts to obtain the vote since the idea of women's suffrage had first been introduced in Washington Territory cannot be denied. Headlines like the *Post-Intelligencer's*

suggested that women's voting had been given to them by men, implying (perhaps to reassure men) that gender hierarchy had been retained and that women continued to benefit from men's magnanimity rather than through any efforts of their own. The truth is, however, that the achievement of women's suffrage in Washington indicated a major "renegotiation of gender boundaries" in the state.[271]

Washington also set the standard for a modern campaign strategy that other states later employed—using several kinds of media, forming coalitions, and conducting a sophisticated, organized campaign. Historian Rebecca Mead characterized the campaign as a "hybrid" that used some older conservative educational strategies as well as more modern media tactics.[272] Washington suffragists passed a symbolic "Votes for Women" banner on to California after the 1910 victory to inspire the 1911 campaign there. By the late 1910s, however, it became evident that the state-by-state strategy had run its course. A national amendment would have to be the path to victory since some states—particularly in the south and northeast—had entrenched opposition to women's suffrage.

UNCLE SAM WELCOMES WASHINGTON TO JOIN WYOMING, COLORADO, UTAH, AND IDAHO IN *VOTES FOR WOMEN*, DECEMBER 1910.

Women Change th

Part 4

Political Landscape

After 1910 Washington's political and legal landscape made a marked turn toward reform as women immediately began to exercise their civic rights. The number of voters nearly doubled.[273] The 1911–12 legislature, dominated by the Progressive spirit and likely influenced by the prospect of women voting, enacted an impressive array of legislation, including direct primary, initiative, referendum, and recall measures; the Seventeenth Amendment (direct election of United States Senators by the people of a state rather than by legislative election or appointment); and labor legislation regarding workmen's compensation and child labor.[274] ★ Women started voting in the same proportion as men. Married women cast 80 percent of women's votes, belying earlier claims that they either would be too

PER
VOTES
V.2, No. 14

The New Citizen

BY Votes for Women PUB. CO.

Copyrighted by Mrs. M. T. B. Hanna

The Magazine that Won Equal Suffrage in Washington

SEATTLE, WASHINGTON, MARCH 1911

We're in POLITICS ourselves

ADVISORY BALLOT

MINISTER

ADVISORY BALLOT

HAS IT COME TO THIS?

FACING PAGE: ALICE PAUL RAISES A TOAST NEAR THE SUFFRAGE AMENDMENT VICTORY FLAG, WHICH HAD ONE STAR FOR EACH STATE NEEDED TO RATIFY THE NATIONAL AMENDMENT.

THIS PAGE: AFTER THE 1910 VICTORY IN WASHINGTON, THE *VOTES FOR WOMEN* NEWSPAPER BECAME *THE NEW CITIZEN.*

busy to vote or would leave it up to their husbands. Famously, women's votes in 1911 swayed
the recall of Seattle mayor Hiram Gill, who was
ousted over accusations that he ran an "open town"
with lax enforcement of gambling and prostitution.[275] Just as Progressives had hoped, the state
legislature, now elected in equal measure by men
and women, continued in a reformist vein between
1913 and 1920, passing legislation regulating liquor,
prostitution, vice, and working conditions, and
promoting the health and morals of women and
children. These measures were viewed as the
"continuing expansion of democracy that had
begun with suffrage."[276] ★ Women did not vote

as a block, contrary to what both pro-suffrage and
anti-suffrage activists had argued (albeit for different
reasons) prior to the victory. Women were informed
voters choosing and studying the issues. They achieved
greater political effectiveness by using their votes in
conjunction with memberships in organizations. Historian Nancy F. Cott noted this tendency after the
federal amendment in 1920 as the forerunner of modern interest-group politics, but it developed after 1910
in Washington as well.[277] ★ In 1916 a joint legislative committee consisting of the State Federation of
Labor, Grange, Farmers Union, and Direct Legislation League worked to defeat legislative challenges to
initiative, referendum, and recall. The State Legislative
Federation, headquartered in Olympia, represented
140 women's clubs and organizations and lobbied for
women's issues, multiplying the effectiveness of the
vote. In 1917 federation representatives worked with
the WCTU on passage of legislation creating a single
standard of adultery for both men and women.[278]
The High School Teachers' League of Seattle and
Representative Frances M. Haskell of Tacoma led
the fight for equal pay for men and women teach-

ers, resulting in legislation passed in 1919. Similarly, the Women's Legislative Council of Washington, organized in 1917, coordinated sixty-six women's clubs throughout the state to advocate for legislation favorable toward "rights for women and children in education, employment, and the penal system."[279] The council operated from 1917 to 1938. It published a newspaper called the *Legislative Counsellor* (originally, the *Legislative Federationist*) to inform members about issues of interest to women. ★ Building on the success of the 1910 campaign, women created new publications and organizations dedicated to women's entry into civic life as informed voters. The suffrage newspaper *Votes for Women* became *The New Citizen*, and its offices housed the Women's Information Bureau.[280] Another post-suffrage periodical, *Western Women's Outlook*, started up in 1911.[281] "Published in the interest of the enfranchised women of the West," *Western Woman Voter* survived intermittently until 1913. Women in Tacoma, Spokane, and Seattle established

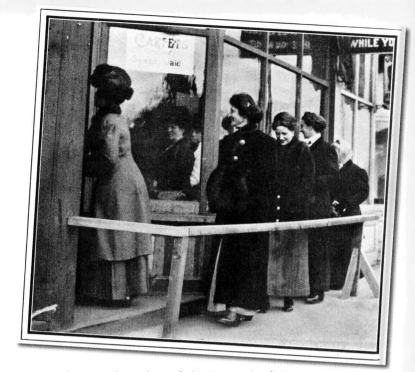

voter education branches of the Council of Women Voters, which spurred activism and encouraged education on issues. ★ The period between 1911 and 1920 was a period of significant legislative changes regarding women's issues abetted by coalitions forged during the suffrage movement among women's clubs and working-class women.[282] Mothers' pensions, the eight-hour workday for women, and Prohibition were part of the Progressive agenda adopted after women attained the ballot. Post-suffrage working-class women increased their role in the labor movement as well as joining with middle-class women in such groups as the King County Legislative Federation to develop an agenda for women's legislative issues.[283] This alliance eventually dissolved because of differences over such issues as radicalism and patriotism before and during World War I.[284]

FACING PAGE: WOMAN WITH A VOTING MACHINE IN TACOMA, 1920S.

THIS PAGE: LARGE NUMBERS OF SEATTLE WOMEN PARTICIPATED IN THE SUCCESSFUL RECALL ELECTION OF HIRAM GILL AS MAYOR OF SEATTLE ON FEBRUARY 7, 1911. FROM C. H. BAILY, "HOW WASHINGTON WOMEN REGAINED THE BALLOT," *PACIFIC MONTHLY*, JULY 1911.

Mothers' Pensions[285]

When the Washington state legislature enacted mothers' pensions in 1913, the victory reflected both the newfound power of women voters and the important role that feminist activists played in creating change in the state. Mothers' pensions were part of the same Progressive ideology that supported the suffrage movement. This maternalistic, civic-housekeeping impulse sought to empower women as a moral force in the public sphere and provided pension payments so mothers could continue to exert moral influence over their children in the home.[286] Based on the philosophy that children were better off with their mothers and not in orphanages, the pension law provided payments to mothers who could not support their children because their husbands had died or abandoned them. The need for pensions became evident after the turn of the twentieth century when the numbers of single mothers rose because of increasing urbanization, abandonment, widowhood, and absence of family support in a more mobile society.

After Illinois became the first state in the country to create mothers' pensions in 1911, a powerful women's group pressured the Washington legislature to follow suit. The Washington Congress of Mothers and Parent-Teacher Associations (WCOM-PTA)—a merger of the Washington Congress of Mothers and the Federation of Parent-Teacher Associations—saw an important opening after the 1912 election. Progressives gained seats in the legislature, women had voting power, and for the first time two women were serving in the state house of representatives. State clubwomen advocated for a wide-ranging reform program for children and families, which included mothers' pensions. The Grange and labor unions joined WCOM-PTA in supporting the measure. Although some charities opposed mothers' pensions, fearing loss of control and influence, the legislation passed, partly because of legislators' sensitivity to the interests of women voters.

At that time the law's provisions were considered liberal although the county juvenile courts, which administered the program, could only provide $15 per month for the first child and $5 for each additional child to mothers in families who had lost the male breadwinner through death or abandonment. The 1915 legislature made provisions more stringent by denying benefits to abandoned women and tightening residency requirements. Although the funds provided much-needed assistance to needy families, administrators sometimes used the law to regulate morality, discriminate against women of color and immigrants, and to spy on women receiving funding. Critics thought it encouraged laziness and dependency. In 1919, women's groups again campaigned to revise the law by calling it a "child maintenance" act. This legislation broadened the categories of those eligible for benefits by including divorced, abandoned, and never-married mothers.

Mothers' pensions were the forerunner of more encompassing reforms. During the 1920s and the Depression, welfare efforts turned to assisting unemployed men. By 1935 the federal Social Security Act created Aid to Dependent Children (ADC). The Washington State ADC followed in 1937. The program title changed to Aid to Families with Dependent Children in 1960, and then in 1996 to Temporary Assistance for Needy Families, which continues today.

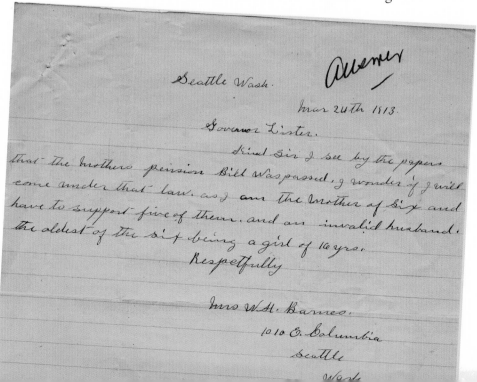

Seattle Wash.

answer

mar 24th 1913.

Governor Lister.

Kind Sir I see by the papers that the mothers pension Bill was passed, I wonder if I will come under that law. as I am the mother of Six and have to support five of them. and an invalid husband. the oldest of the six being a girl of 16 yrs.

Respectfully

Mrs W.H. Barnes.
1010 E. Columbia
Seattle
Wash.

The Eight-hour Day

Often called the "Waitresses Bill," the eight-hour workday for women, enacted in 1911, honored the efforts of Alice Lord, who founded the pioneering Seattle Waitresses Union in 1900. Legislators had enacted the ten-hour day in 1901, but Lord sought a six-day workweek and eight-hour workday for women. She tirelessly lobbied Olympia for improvements for working women. After 1910 women's clubs and former suffragists, including May Arkwright Hutton and Emma Smith DeVoe, supported the cause of the reduced workday for women, reciprocating the support given by labor and Alice Lord to the suffrage cause in 1910. Everett representative John Campbell, later dubbed "8-Hour Jack," championed the legislation, presenting a mammoth petition for the bill.[287] However, businesses, chambers of commerce, and even some working women opposed the bill for its protectionist tone as limiting job options and pay for female employees.[288] The

compromise bill finally passed, excluding women who worked for food industries dependent on timely processing of perishable foods.[289]

Lord continued to fight for a six-day workweek, which was established in Washington in 1920. When Lord died in 1940 members of Seattle's labor movement mourned her loss. Bob Harlin, her memorialist, said, "In earlier days Seattle was a rough town. When girls came here, whether they got a job or walked the streets destitute was nobody's business but their own. But many such one has she helped. Many of you do not appreciate the fight that had to be waged in those old days . . . ." The minister officiating at her funeral noted, "She left the conditions for working women far better than she found them."[290]

FACING PAGE: ONE OF THE MANY LETTERS FROM DESTITUTE MOTHERS SEEKING ASSISTANCE FROM THE MOTHERS' PENSIONS PROGRAM AMONG GOVERNOR ERNEST LISTER'S PAPERS.

ABOVE: WAITRESSES ASSOCIATION OF SEATTLE AUTOMOBILE FLOAT IN THE 1905 SEATTLE LABOR PARADE.

RIGHT: ALICE LORD (1877-1940), A TIRELESS ADVOCATE FOR WORKING WOMEN, AT THE OFFICE OF THE WAITRESSES ASSOCIATION OF SEATTLE, C. 1905.

Prohibition

*C*oncerns about alcohol were widespread in the late nineteenth century, but Washington voters had turned down prohibition along with women's suffrage in 1889. By the early twentieth century, however, new brewing technologies and the coming of the railroads made for easier distribution of alcoholic beverages to every community. This—coupled with Progressive ideals about the influence of individual health on social well-being and with more vocal, better organized prohibition groups—resulted in increased opposition to saloons. A wide-ranging local-option bill passed the legislature in 1909 in which 30 percent of registered voters in towns, cities, and unincorporated county areas could petition for an election to vote dry. Legislators also restricted saloon operations—e.g., keeping minors and women out of saloons and providing for unrestricted views of saloon interiors.[291] Seventy local-option elections were on ballots around the state along with the women's suffrage amendment in November 1910, and in many cases local-option results garnered larger headlines than the women's victory. Although pressed for further action, the 1911 legislature failed to impose more restrictions.

With the addition of initiative and referendum to the Washington constitution in 1912, anti-saloon forces circulated a prohibition proposition—Initiative Measure 3—and secured enough signatures for the measure to be on the 1914 ballot. Many of the same groups that supported women's suffrage—Progressives, the Grange, the WCTU, and churches—also backed prohibition in Washington.[292] An overwhelming 94.6 percent of the eligible voters in Washington cast their ballots on the initiative for a state constitutional prohibition amendment, which won by a margin of 18,632 votes.[293] The law, which took effect January 1, 1916, closed saloons but allowed individuals to secure as much as two quarts of liquor or twelve quarts of beer every twenty days by permit from county auditors. Lawmakers in 1917 enacted a stricter, "bone-dry" law that ended the permit system of obtaining alcohol, an act upheld by voter referendum in 1918. The Eighteenth Amendment for national prohibition went into effect in 1920. Washington voted by initiative for repeal of state liquor laws in 1932. National Prohibition was revoked in 1933.

The National Suffrage Campaign

Shortly after the Washington suffrage victory in 1910, Emma Smith DeVoe spearheaded the creation of the National Council of Women Voters (NCWV), a nonpartisan coalition of women from voting states. DeVoe organized this separate group partly in response to her rebuff by NAWSA at their 1909 national convention in Seattle. She also wanted to show the dissatisfaction of western states with the organization.[294] The goals of the NCWV were to create an educational organization for women voters, to lobby for legislation, and to extend women's suffrage nationally. DeVoe envisioned an evolving group that would add members from states as they enacted women's suffrage. Creation of this coalition highlighted the differing strategies among western suffragists and NAWSA and enfranchised women who desired to take a more active role in the national campaign.[295]

DeVoe successfully encouraged Idaho governor James Brady to call a meeting to form the NCWV. The meeting took place on January 11, 1911, in Tacoma. Brady asked each suffrage state to appoint a recognized suffragist as a council delegate. Idaho appointed Margaret S. Roberts; Wyoming, Zell Hart Deming; Colorado, Mary C. C. Bradford; Utah, Susan Young Gates; and Washington, Virginia Wilson Mason. DeVoe was named president at the initial meeting in Tacoma, which was sparsely attended because a snowstorm kept Wyoming and Utah delegates from attending. Anna Howard Shaw said she recognized DeVoe's ambitions to control NCWV and Cora Smith Eaton's tactics in supporting her as similar to those they had used to take control at the 1909 WESA convention.[296] DeVoe and Eaton's actions elicited outcry from opponents in Washington State, with Hutton noting, "It looks like Tammany to me."[297] Other groups, including Washington's Federation of Labor, Grange, Farmer's Union, and women's clubs also condemned DeVoe's actions, which appeared to have gained her a "rail-roaded" presidency.[298] From its headquarters in Tacoma, the NCWV, however, moved forward as part of the national campaign for women's suffrage.

At Last

Signaling a change in national tactics away from the less militant NAWSA strategies, Alice Paul had formed the Congressional Union (CU) in April 1913 with the singular goal of a constitutional amendment guaranteeing women the right to vote. The NCWV soon joined forces with the CU. Paul and her colleague Lucy Burns had worked with militant suffragettes in England and wanted to implement similar tactics in the United States. Instead of asking for the vote, they believed in demanding women's suffrage. Paul was riding a momentous wave of publicity, which had been gathering force in the wake of the massive March 3, 1913, pro-suffrage parade in Washington, D.C., which she had organized as leader of NAWSA's Congressional Committee just prior to President Woodrow Wilson's inauguration.

FACING PAGE, TOP: THE HATCHET BECAME A SYMBOL OF PROHIBITION, HARKENING TO CARRY A. NATION'S USE OF A HATCHET ON SALOONS AND WHISKEY BARRELS AROUND THE TURN OF THE 20TH CENTURY.

FACING PAGE, BOTTOM: PROHIBITIONIST PAMPHLET URGING WOMEN TO VOTE FOR PRO-PROHIBITION CANDIDATES IN 1912 AND FOR PROHIBITION LEGISLATION IN 1914.

THIS PAGE: *THE SUFFRAGIST*, PUBLISHED BY THE NATIONAL WOMAN'S PARTY, CELEBRATED THE PASSAGE OF THE 19TH AMENDMENT BY CONGRESS IN JUNE 1919. THE LAST OF THE REQUIRED 36 STATES RATIFIED IT IN AUGUST 1920, AND IT BECAME LAW ON AUGUST 26, 1920.

Although the parade was a public relations coup, it in many ways symbolized the divide that had been growing within NAWSA over strategy.

Emma Smith DeVoe relished the CU alliance because of her split with NAWSA and, at first, concurred with their more militant tactics. Cora Smith Eaton, a veteran of the Washington campaign,  joined DeVoe's activism. An NCWV affiliate, Eaton married Judson King in 1912 and moved to Washington, D.C. As chair of the NCWV Congressional Committee, she often testified before Congress on behalf of the enfranchised women of Washington and the NCWV, sometimes joined by DeVoe. King headed a delegation of nine members of the NCWV, which met with President Wilson on March 31, 1913. They were only the third group to meet with the president after his inauguration.[299] King also organized a suffrage amendment demonstration in Hyattsville, Maryland, on July 31, 1913. Suffragists from all over the country rendezvoused there for a car caravan to Washington, D.C., where they presented petitions to their congressmen.[300]

Consisting as it did of a large block of voting women, the NCWV appealed to elected officials. The CU, which held elected officials responsible for the enactment of women's suffrage, thus saw the NCWV as a valuable ally. In 1914, as part of its overall strategy, the CU sent representatives to Washington State to work against electing Democrats to Congress—a move that was generally opposed by Washington women voters who had steered away from party politics in the 1910 victory.[301] In April 1916 the CU again sent national organizers to enfranchised states on a "Suffrage Special" train to garner support from voting women to pressure Congress for a federal amendment. CU representative Harriet Stanton Blatch, Elizabeth Cady Stanton's daughter, gave a speech in Seattle and was part of a procession of 150 cars that toured the city decked out in purple, white, and gold banners. CU delegate Lucy Burns scattered leaflets over the city from an airplane. Envoys went on to Bellingham and later to Spokane, where they planted a tree in honor of May Arkwright Hutton.[302]

ABOVE: AT A NATIONWIDE SUFFRAGE MEETING IN NEW YORK CITY IN 1912, DR. ANNA HOWARD SHAW (IN DEAN'S GARB) LEADS DELEGATES FROM OTHER STATES DOWN MANHATTAN'S FIFTH AVENUE.

LEFT: STALWART SUFFRAGIST ALICE PAUL (1885-1977), C. 1910.

After the 1915 NCWV National Convention DeVoe began to migrate away from her CU affiliation back toward NAWSA. DeVoe's longtime colleague, Carrie Chapman Catt, regained the presidency of NAWSA, unseating Anna Howard Shaw in 1915. Catt changed NAWSA's focus from state-by-state victories to the ratification of a national amendment, although she still included a role for individual states in her "Winning Plan," adopted in 1916. By March 1917 Paul had changed the name of the Congressional Union to the National Woman's Party (NWP) and made it independent of NAWSA. The NWP used marches, protests, and pickets at the White House to bring attention to the cause. Several of the picketing women were arrested, beaten, and force-fed.[303] Preferring non-partisanship in the suffrage campaign, Catt and NAWSA generally opposed the NWP's militant tactics as well as its policy of holding political parties accountable for a women's suffrage victory.

Colors and Images of the Suffrage Movement

Women in Washington adopted the color orange in honor of Judge Orange Jacobs, a prominent suffrage supporter who served on the Territorial Supreme Court and as a delegate to Congress. Early suffragists wore orange ribbons in his honor.[304] The *Washington Women's Cook Book* published for the 1909–1910 campaign used orange lettering on its cover. ☆ When American suffragists returned from working in England, they brought back the tricolors of the purple, white, and green to symbolize loyalty, purity, and hope. They later substituted gold for green. Symbolic of the Kansas state sunflower, yellow or gold came from the failed Kansas suffrage campaign in 1867, conducted by Susan B. Anthony and Elizabeth Cady Stanton. Yellow was adopted as an official color at the American Woman Suffrage Association in 1876. Gold was later paired with "Votes for Women," the primary suffrage slogan. In Washington the signature pennant pin during the 1909–1910 campaign was green, probably for the Evergreen State, with the slogan "Votes for Women" in gold lettering. ☆ Generally, suffragists wore white, symbolizing purity for women. This was part of a long tradition among women demonstrators, including those active in the Prohibition movement, who wore white to signal that, although they might be *in* the streets, they were not *of* the streets. Sometimes ridiculed by men for their appearance in public marches, temperance workers donned white clothing to symbolize their personal integrity and the rightness of their cause; suffragists followed their lead.[305] ☆ Postcards and cartoons ridiculing suffrage often showed henpecked husbands minding the children and performing chores traditionally considered "women's work."

THE AWAKENING

Suffragists themselves employed heroic symbols for their cause, including iconic images of democracy and equality. They also used icons of heralds and angels, hearkening back to the goddesses of Liberty and Justice and the female personification of the United States—the goddess Columbia. The suffrage movement employed the slogans and symbolism of "going forward into the light" to signify progress for women.

Enlightenment marched from west to east. This 1915 image, "The Awakening," by Hy Mayer, illustrates western states leading the way to women's suffrage.

During World War I NAWSA withdrew from suffrage work to support the war effort, but the NWP continued its militant tactics, likening President Wilson to the German Kaiser for supporting a war for "democracy" in Europe while American women lacked a political voice at home.[306] Catt believed that women's service in home-front activities during

World War I—such as food preservation, war bond sales, and Red Cross work—would enhance their case for equal citizenship.[307]

Finally, in June 1919, after intense pressure from both NWP and NAWSA, Congress passed the Nineteenth Amendment to the U.S. Constitution and sent it to the states for ratification. Washington was the penultimate of thirty-six states needed to ratify the amendment and the last enfranchised state to take action. DeVoe and Catt pressured a reluctant Governor Louis Hart to call a special legislative session. Hart feared that other matters would barrage the legislature in a special session but eventually agreed to call the legislators together in March 1920. Pierce County representative Frances Haskell, the fourth woman elected to the Washington legislature, introduced the resolution, stating:

UPPER LEFT: LUCY BURNS AND LIEUTENANT TERAH MARONEY IN HYDROPLANE, PREPARING TO FLY OVER SEATTLE TO DISTRIBUTE SUFFRAGIST LITERATURE DURING THE 1916 SUFFRAGE SPECIAL TOUR.

BELOW: THIRD DEPUTATION TO PRESIDENT WILSON, COMPOSED OF VOTING WOMEN, LED BY DR. CORA SMITH KING (THIRD FROM LEFT) OF WASHINGTON STATE IN 1913.

This is a very important hour in the history of our state and nation, for we have met here in special session the 22nd day of March, in the year of our Lord 1920, to ratify the federal suffrage amendment and to prove to the world the greatness of our Evergreen state, which is not determined by the number of acres that it contains nor by the number of its population, but by the character of its men and women who today are extending to all the women of America the privilege of the ballot.[308]

Governor Hart, Speaker of the House Fred Adams, and Emma Smith DeVoe shared the dais in the house of representatives, and by special resolution DeVoe expressed her thanks to the legislature. In the senate veteran suffragist Carrie Hill shared the podium with President of the Senate Philip H. Carlyon of Olympia. Both houses cast a unanimous vote to ratify the Nineteenth Amendment—the twelfth state in which no one voted against it.[309] Tennessee was the final state needed to ratify the amendment, which codified that "the right of citizens of the United States to vote shall not be denied or abridged by the Unites States or by any State on account of sex."[310] The amendment took effect August 26, 1920.

League of Women Voters

*E*ven before the victory in August 1920, Catt envisioned creating a League of Women Voters (LWV). DeVoe and the NCWV may have influenced Catt in its creation.[311] At the NAWSA convention in March 1919, DeVoe merged the NCWV with the LWV, making the action official on January 6, 1920, and

---

Citizenship and Voting

Not all women in the United States could vote after passage of Washington's suffrage act or the Nineteenth Amendment, since many groups were restricted from becoming citizens, a qualification for voting. Native American women, who were excluded from voting even after passage of the suffrage amendments in 1910 and 1920, finally achieved the right to vote in 1924 when Congress passed the Indian Citizenship Act, which extended U.S. citizenship to Native Americans. Asian women faced other citizenship restrictions. By national law, native-born Asian residents were considered citizens by 1898. Immigrant Asians, however, were denied citizenship well into the mid twentieth century. By 1943 Chinese immigrants could be naturalized and vote; immigrants from India received the same rights starting in 1946; and Japanese and other Asians in 1952.[312] ☆ Some voters faced racist barriers. Although black women achieved the right to vote in 1910 in Washington and in 1920 nationally, barriers remained. In 1964, largely in response to widespread racial discrimination in the South, the Twenty-fourth Amendment to the U.S. Constitution prohibited states from charging poll tax. Most significant was passage in 1965 of the Voting Rights Act, which ended practices that disenfranchised black voters and broadened and guaranteed voting rights specifically to minorities. The Twenty-sixth Amendment lowered the voting age to eighteen in 1971. To make Washington law consistent with national standards, the state amended its constitution in 1974 to lower the voting age to eighteen and removed the 1896 provision requiring voters to read and speak English.[313]

Nettie Chiang (1876–1914) (later James) of Olympia. She and her husband Jim Ah Toone came to Olympia from Seattle after 1889 and operated the Gold Bar Restaurant in the 1890s.

served on the first LWV council. Nellie Mitchell Fick of Seattle was temporary chair, and Teresa Griswold of Seattle became permanent chair of the LWV in Washington after the merger. The league continues today, describing itself as "a nonpartisan political organization [that] encourages informed and active participation in government, works to increase understanding of major public policy issues, and influences public policy through education and advocacy to inform and inspire educated and active citizen participation."[314]

Expanding Roles for Women

*D*uring World War I Washington women served in several capacities on the home front, including the Council of National Defense and the National League for Woman's Service.[315] Other women resisted the war effort and joined the international peace movement through the Woman's Peace Party and other groups. Washington women

appeared to be more equal partners with men in the home-front war effort because of their enfranchisement, unlike in other states where women were sometimes marginalized because they had no obvious political voice.[316]

During the war, Washington women organized under the auspices of the Minute Women, part of the Washington Council of Defense. They sold Liberty Loan Bonds and promoted conservation of sugar, flour, and cereals.[317] The Minute Women also took on the job of conducting censuses and distributing war-related information.[318]

The National League for Woman's Service (NLWS) taught women skills like telegraphy, automobile driving, and running elevators, and instructed women on the use of rifles for home defense or patrol work. The NLWS raised money for European victims, including raising thousands of dollars to provide chickens for war-torn France. During the war women also cooperated with the Young Men's Christian Association (YMCA), helping soldiers and sailors and providing "wholesome" entertainment. Women joined the Red Cross to knit socks and scarves, make dressings, roll bandages, and sew hospital and refugee garments. Women helped gather crops in Washington and canned fruits and vegetables for hospitalized soldiers.[319]

After the war, the Minute Women worked for veterans and refugees with the American Legion and other groups. They continued to serve the needs of wounded veterans and their families, supporting veterans in hospitals at American Lake, Bremerton, and Port Townsend. In those postwar years labor strife in Washington took center stage, and many women joined in the conflict. Anna Louise Strong, a former Seattle School Board member, was a leader in the Seattle General Strike of 1919 and, like many other women, became associated with the International Workers of the World and other radical labor groups.[320]

Women and women's groups continued in their mission of municipal housekeeping and advocacy for changes in other areas related to home and family. However, after the success of the Nineteenth Amendment, many women who had joined together in the suffrage movement turned to more individualist forms of feminism. "Whereas the woman movement stood for selflessness in service to the cause," historian Ellen Carol Dubois explains, after women got the vote, "feminism stood for self-development as the route to women's emancipation."[321] Far from forming a uniform voting bloc after 1920 as so many anti-suffrage activists had feared, women and women's groups instead worked for a wide variety of causes, including environmental preservation and conservation, the peace movement, prohibition, and labor reform. Often, women who had fought side-by-side for suffrage became adversaries once the vote had been won.

Bertha Landes's election as Seattle mayor in 1926 symbolized women's achievements in political and civic life after the Nineteenth Amendment, and demonstrated the importance of having the support of voting clubwomen in Seattle elections. The first woman elected mayor of a major American city, Landes was former president of the Washington State General Federation of Women's Clubs and received support from women's clubs statewide.[322] She strove for reform and fiscal stability during her two-year term but was defeated for a second term, likely in part because of her gender.[323]

During the Great Depression, women participated in New Deal projects and programs and organized for relief efforts in their own communities. Washington State continued to be a leader in reforms for women when the legislature enacted landmark legislation in 1932 by implementing a minimum wage law for women, which the U.S. Supreme Court upheld in 1937 in *West Coast Hotel v. Parrish.*[324]

Washington women also played a central role in the national effort during World War II. Working at shipyards in Vancouver and Tacoma, and building planes for Boeing, they earned the epithet "Rosie the Riveter" for working in manual labor positions that were once considered only suitable for men. In addition to civilian jobs, women enlisted in all branches of the armed forces, serving both stateside and abroad in Women Airforce Service Pilots (WASP), Women's Army Corps (WAC), and Women Accepted for Volunteer Emergency Service (WAVES).[325]

As they had done in World War I, women organized on the home front, helping with bond drives, promoting food economy, contributing such items as nylon stockings for war matériel, and staffing United Service Organizations (USOS). They worked as aircraft spotters in western Washington and served on "filter boards" that compiled information about sightings of enemy aircraft approaching from the Pacific.

Japanese women living in the coastal areas of Washington had a very different experience of the war. They and their families were sent to internment camps, and in many cases the disruption to their lives lasted beyond the war's duration.

After the war many women who had worked in high-paying war jobs were forced out by returning veterans. Some returned to more traditional roles in the home. However, many women continued to work outside their homes and advocate for women's rights, and by the mid twentieth century women's lives and roles were changing again.

FACING PAGE: ARTIST HOWARD CHANDLER CHRISTY (1873-1952) CREATED THIS ALLEGORICAL FIGURE IN 1919 TO PROMOTE VICTORY LIBERTY LOAN BONDS IN SUPPORT OF WORLD WAR I. THE "HONOR ROLL" CONSISTS OF LAST NAMES FROM DIFFERENT ETHNIC GROUPS.

ABOVE: ATTENDEES AT THE 1927 CONVENTION OF THE WASHINGTON FEDERATION OF WOMEN'S CLUBS IN WALLA WALLA.

Modern Washi
Pursue Equal

ERA
ERA
ER

Equal Rights Amendment Rally on the Capitol Steps, 1971-1
General Photo Collection, Washington State Archives.

Part 5

Women's Rights

Despite an emphasis on domesticity and media perceptions, women—particularly older, married women—entered the workforce in growing numbers after 1947, an increase of nearly 10 percent during that period.[326] According to historian Glenda Riley, women also continued to participate in organizations that fostered leadership skills.[327] Writers Leila J. Rupp and Verta Taylor wrote that the period between 1945 and the 1960s can be understood "as a link in the chain stretching from the early women's rights movement of the 1840s to the women's movement of the 1980s."[328] ★ During the postwar period it was generally white, well-educated women who worked in a variety of women's rights groups, advocating for the Equal Rights Amendment and elevating women to policy-decision positions that recognized the importance of women's history. The National Woman's Party (NWP), historically active in the suffrage movement, supported these issues. Groups such as Business and Professional Women,

THIS PAGE: BUTTONS AND STICKERS WERE USED ON BOTH SIDES OF THE ERA DEBATE.

FACING PAGE: WASHINGTON WOMEN RALLY FOR THE STATE EQUAL RIGHTS AMENDMENT IN FRONT OF THE CAPITOL BUILDING IN OLYMPIA.

General Federation of Women's Clubs, American Association of University Women, National Association of Colored Women, Zonta, Soroptimist, Altrusa, and others joined with the NWP in the postwar years to accomplish these goals. Women often joined one or more of these groups, building coalitions, keeping the feminist movement alive until its resurgence later in the century.[329] ★ Inspired by Civil Rights and antiwar activism, "second wave" feminism emerged as a powerful social force in the 1960s. President John F. Kennedy established the Presidential Commission on the Status of Women in 1961 and Washington governor Albert Rossellini established the Washington Commission on the Status of Women in 1963. The state commission continued under Governor Dan Evans's administrations, and in 1971 Evans created its successor, the Washington State Women's Council, which Governor Dixy Lee Ray dismantled in 1978 following passage of a statewide referendum expressing disapproval of a plan to make the council a permanent state agency.[330]

Betty Freidan's book, *The Feminine Mystique*, published in 1963, was a national catalyst for the women's movement, setting the stage for the next phase. Like their nineteenth-century counterparts, second-wave feminists perceived women's relegation to the domestic sphere as oppressive and turned to activism to garner support for equality. Among many other issues, women in Washington campaigned both for and against the state and national equal rights amendments, filed suit to achieve equality in funding for women's athletics, and pursued comparable compensation for female state employees.[331]

The Equal Rights Amendment

Through the efforts and organization of many women's groups, Washington voters passed the Equal Rights Amendment (HJR 61) to the Washington State Constitution in 1972. The amendment reads: "Equality of rights and responsibility under the law shall not be denied or abridged on account of sex." Supporters included the Committee for HJR 61—Washington's Equal Rights Amendment, co-chaired by Betty Fletcher and Glenn Terrell, then president of Washington State University; the National Organization for Women; American Association of University Women; and the League of Women Voters. Many women's groups opposed the amendment, including HOW (Happiness of Women) and the League of Housewives, who argued that the legislation was harmful to families and that "women's lib" would both undermine traditional values and remove gender-based protections for women.

The hotly contested amendment passed by a narrow margin of 3,369 votes. Materially advancing equality of the sexes, the legislation mandated changes to over 130 Washington laws relating to discrimination against men or women in insurance, credit, the right

FACING PAGE: FEMINISTS MARCH IN WASHINGTON, D.C., IN 1978 ON THE ANNIVERSARY OF THE NINETEENTH AMENDMENT'S ADOPTION. THE BANNER STATES THE WORDING OF SECTION ONE OF THE FEDERAL EQUAL RIGHTS AMENDMENT.

THIS PAGE: PRESIDENT JOHN F. KENNEDY SIGNS THE EQUAL PAY ACT ON JUNE 10, 1963, MAKING IT ILLEGAL TO PAY WOMEN LOWER WAGES FOR THE SAME WORK STRICTLY ON THE BASIS OF THEIR SEX. WASHINGTON'S CONGRESSIONAL REPRESENTATIVES CATHERINE MAY (FIFTH FROM LEFT), A COSPONSOR OF THE LEGISLATION, AND JULIA BUTLER HANSEN (FAR RIGHT) WITNESSED THE SIGNING.

to sue, child support, and labor.[332] Washington is one of several states to have enacted a constitutional amendment prohibiting discrimination on the basis of sex in all areas of public life; other states have protected similar rights through legislation.[333]

Believing that passage of the Nineteenth Amendment was just the first step in ensuring women's political and social equality, suffragist and president of the National Woman's Party Alice Paul first proposed an equal rights amendment to the U.S. Constitution in 1923. Second-wave feminists, frustrated that women still had not achieved equality with men half a century later, revitalized the national ERA campaign in the 1970s. Congress passed the amendment—"equality of rights under the law shall not be denied or abridged by the United States or by any state on account of sex"[334]—in 1972 and forwarded it to the states for ratification. The Washington legislature ratified it in 1973. Many of the same groups in Washington that had worked for and against the state ERA were active in the campaign for national ratification.

Washington is one of thirty-five states to have ratified the federal amendment. Congress extended the federal ratification deadline to 1982,

Ellensburg International Women's Year Conference

The Washington State International Women's Year (IWY) Conference in 1977, a state meeting preceding the National Women's Conference in Houston the same year, brought into focus the conflicts among women related to the feminist movement and differences of opinion about women's roles. During the four-day event in July, women from all over the state debated issues and elected delegates to the national convention.[335] ☆ Governor Albert Rossellini had established the Washington Commission on the Status of Women in the early 1960s. Governor Dan Evans created its successor—the Washington State Women's Council—in 1971 to identify and make recommendations to state government regarding women's issues. The council successfully advocated in the early 1970s for the Washington Equal Rights Amendment and community-property law changes. The council also conducted conferences and hearings, and worked for other legislative changes to benefit women. The state legislature in 1977 authorized the council to become a permanent state agency as the Washington State Women's Commission. ☆ After the Ellensburg IWY Conference, attendee Susan Roylance and other women who opposed the conduct and outcomes of the conference, especially its pro-ERA tenor, formed Women for Integrity in the Nation (WIN). WIN gathered signatures for Referendum 40, which opposed designation of the council as a state agency. They said the council represented only a liberal feminist viewpoint, not the perspectives of all Washington women. ☆ The referendum, worded in favor of creating a commission, lost by a large margin, 240,000–600,000. The defeat was a victory for antifeminist women, but it also reflected an anti-government sentiment and some confusion about the measure. Reacting to the Referendum 40 vote, Governor Dixy Lee Ray disbanded the Women's Council in 1978.[336] ☆ After the council was eliminated, many felt the loss of an advocacy voice for issues related to women. Several women's organizations formed a new legislative lobbying group—Washington Women United (WWU)—in 1978. Although WWU required its members to support the ERA, the organization provided a voice for different groups to lobby for legislative action around women's issues, including comparable worth. WWU ceased to exist in the 1990s when the political climate for women's issues generally improved and individual women's groups hired their own lobbyists.

"...to form a more perfect union..."

Washington State Conference For
WOMEN

July 8 ~ 10, 1977
Central Washington State College, Ellensburg

Scholarships Available
Registration Deadline June 1
For Further Information Contact:

Grass Roots Involvement For All Women:
Workshops - Multi-Media Entertainment
Speakouts - Films - Dialogue
Final Report To President Carter

Sponsored By National Commission For International Women's Year

Poster promoting Washington's 1977 IWY Conference in Ellensburg.

but it expired without being passed by the required thirty-eight states. The amendment has been reintroduced unsuccessfully in every Congress since 1982. Whether states that have already ratified would still count toward the amendment if it is reauthorized remains debatable.

Title IX

*A*chieving equality in athletics and education has long been of concern to feminists nationally and in the state of Washington. Young women's lives changed dramatically in 1972 when they gained equal access to athletics and academic programs in high school and college via Title IX, an amendatory section of the Civil Rights Act of 1964. The Title IX law has been renamed the Patsy T. Mink Equal Opportunity in Education Act to honor the Hawaii congresswoman who championed its passage. The law states: "No person in the United States shall, on the basis of sex, be excluded from participation in, or denied the benefits of, or be subjected to discrimination under any educational program or activity receiving federal assistance." Washington State enacted similar language for state-funded school activities in 1975.

Despite enactment of Title IX, room for improvement remained in sports-funding equity. In 1979

students and coaches at Washington State University filed suit under the state's ERA amendment in *Blair v. Washington State University*. The plaintiffs' strategy was to improve support for women's college sports by including men's football in determining parity funding. Although they lost the suit at first, the decision was reversed on appeal in 1987 when the state supreme court ruled in favor of the plaintiffs, increasing funding for women's sports in all four-year state colleges and universities.[337]

WASHINGTON STATE UNIVERSITY VS. UNIVERSITY OF SOUTHERN CALIFORNIA, 2008. THE PASSAGE OF TITLE IX GAVE A TREMENDOUS BOOST TO WOMEN'S HIGH SCHOOL AND COLLEGE SPORTS.

Reproductive Rights

In 1970 Washington voters passed a referendum allowing legalized abortion during early pregnancy with some restrictions. Many groups advocated for the legislation, including Pro-Choice Washington, Planned Parenthood, church groups, the League of Women Voters, and the American Association of University Women. Human Life, Voice for the Unborn, Catholics United for the Faith, and other groups opposed the referendum. Washington was the first state to put the issue on the ballot, although other states had enacted legislation permitting abortions. The ballot issue developed from a study group that worked with Senator Joel Pritchard, chief legislative sponsor of the bill. The u.s. Supreme Court ruling in *Roe v. Wade* in 1973 took precedence over Washington law. In 1991, Washington voters approved by a small margin a referendum that repealed the 1970 law and instituted the current language, which declares that "every individual possesses a fundamental right of privacy with respect to personal reproductive decisions."[338]

Comparable Worth

Equal pay for equal work has long been a feminist rallying cry. By implementing comparable worth in state employee salaries, Washington became a leader among states in upholding women's right to equitable pay. Citing inequities between the salaries paid to men and women employees whose jobs appeared to have equal value, the Washington State Federation of State Employees sent a letter to then Governor Dan Evans in 1973 asking for action to remedy the problem. In response, Evans directed the Higher Education Personnel Board and the Department of Personnel to initiate a study to compare salaries for jobs requiring equivalent skill and responsibilities. This led to a more substantial statewide study in 1974, which found that women overall received about 20 percent lower pay than men for comparable employment.

After several years waiting for the state to remedy pay inequities identified in the Department of Personnel report, the Washington State Federation of State Employees filed suit in U.S. District Court in 1982. The court found the State of Washington guilty of discrimination and required the state to implement a comparable worth program. The case was reversed on appeal in 1985, but the state and the union soon negotiated a settlement, which the legislature ratified in 1986, instituting annual equitable adjustments until 1992. About 35,000 state employees benefited, each receiving a part of the $482 million settlement.[339]

Elected Washington Women

Washington's remarkable record of electing women to public office reflects a legacy of feminist activism. Although women had been elected to serve as county school superintendents as early as 1875, the Washington legislature

ABOVE, LEFT: BUTTONS FROM THE 1980S COMPARABLE WORTH CAMPAIGN IN WASHINGTON.

passed a law in 1890 disqualifying women from public office. An early exception was made in 1895 when the legislature authorized women to serve on school boards, the state board of education, and as school superintendents. Surprisingly, the legislature did not formally repeal its general prohibition until 1963.

After the state enacted women's suffrage in 1910, Washington women began to run for office in ever-increasing numbers. Elected in 1912 and serving in the 1913 state house of representatives, Frances C. Axtell from Bellingham and Nena J. Croake from Tacoma were the first two women to serve in the Washington State Legislature. Reba Hurn from Spokane was in 1923 the first woman elected to the state senate. Josephine Corliss Preston, elected in 1912 as superintendent of public instruction, was the first woman to serve in a statewide office. From the mid 1960s on, women of color began holding office as well, with Representative Marjorie Pitter King (appointed in 1965 to fill an unexpired term) being Washington's first black female legislator, Representative Velma Veloria the first Filipina American (elected 1992), and Senator Margarita Prentice (house, 1988; senate, 1993) the first Latina. As of this writing, over 230 women have served in the Washington legislature since 1913.

For almost 25 years Washington has consistently been a leader in electing women to the state legislature. From 1993 to 2004 Washington led the nation in the percentage of female state legislators. In 1999 and 2000 Washington boasted the highest percentage of female legislators in the nation's history, with women making up 41 percent of its legislators. In 2009 women comprised approximately one-third of the state's legislators.

Washington women have served as superintendent of public instruction, secretary of state, attorney general, commissioner of public lands, and insurance commissioner. Elected in 1981, Carolyn Dimmick was the first woman to serve on the Washington State Supreme Court. In 2003, when Supreme Court Justice Mary Fairhurst took the oath of office, the Washington State Supreme Court had a female majority for the first time in its history, and it was the first state with a nine-member court to have a majority of women justices. Nine women have served on the state supreme court over time. Washington women have also held elected positions on local school boards, local courts, special purpose districts, city councils, county commissions and councils, and as county executives throughout the state's history. As of 2008, eight of thirty federally recognized tribes in Washington had women chairpersons.

Washington has elected two women governors: Dixy Lee Ray (1977-1981) and the current governor, Chris Gregoire, first elected in 2004 and now serving a second term. Only thirty women have been elected governor of any state. In 2005 Washington became the first state to have a female governor (Chris Gregoire) and two female U.S. senators (Patty Murray and Maria Cantwell) serving simultaneously. Senator Murray, first elected in 1992 and reelected in 1998 and 2004; and Senator Cantwell, elected in 2000 and reelected in 2006, are the state's first two female U.S. senators. Seven women from Washington have served in the U.S. House of Representatives. Serving from 1959 to 1970, Catherine May was the first woman in Congress from Washington, elected from the Fourth Congressional District east of the Cascades.[340] Other women elected to Congress include Julia Butler Hansen (1960–1974); Jolene Unsoeld (1989–1995); Maria Cantwell (1993–1995); Linda Smith (1995–1999); Jennifer Dunn, (1993–2005); and Cathy McMorris Rodgers (elected in 2004 and reelected in 2006 and 2008).[341]

Contemporary Washington Women

*D*ebate continues across a broad political spectrum over the role of women and women's rights in Washington. As women have gained prominence in business, professions, philanthropy, science, sports, and almost every other area of public and private life, those changes and opportunities hearken back to 1910, when Washington women entered a sphere of citizenship, activism, and influence that had been unattainable before they became full participants in the civic life of Washington and the nation. Women's voices and their viewpoints, expressed through their votes, have shaped and continue to shape the hisory of Washington.

POLITICAL FIRSTS FOR WASHINGTON (LEFT TO RIGHT): NENA JOLIDON CROAKE (1856?–1934) FROM TACOMA WAS ONE OF FIRST TWO WOMEN, ALONG WITH FRANCES AXTELL OF BELLINGHAM, ELECTED TO THE WASHINGTON STATE LEGISLATURE IN 1912. JOSEPHINE CORLISS PRESTON (1873–1958) BECAME THE FIRST WOMAN ELECTED TO STATEWIDE OFFICE IN WASHINGTON, SERVING AS SUPERINTENDENT OF PUBLIC INSTRUCTION FROM 1913 TO 1928. LABOR ACTIVIST VELMA VELORIA, THE FIRST FILIPINA AMERICAN TO SERVE IN THE STATE LEGISLATURE, REPRESENTED THE SEATTLE AREA FOR TWELVE YEARS AFTER HER ELECTION IN 1992. MARIA CANTWELL WAS ELECTED TO THE U.S. SENATE IN 2000 AND RE-ELECTED IN 2006, HAVING SERVED IN THE STATE LEGISLATURE FROM 1987 TO 1993 AND IN THE U.S. HOUSE OF REPRESENTATIVES FROM 1993 TO 1995. CHRIS GREGOIRE BECAME WASHINGTON'S SECOND WOMAN GOVERNOR, ELECTED IN 2004 AND RE-ELECTED IN 2008, HAVING SERVED AS THE STATE'S FIRST FEMALE ATTORNEY GENERAL FROM 1993 TO 2004. SENATOR PATTY MURRAY WAS ELECTED TO THE STATE SENATE FOR A FOUR-YEAR TERM IN 1988 AND THEN BECAME THE STATE'S FIRST FEMALE U.S. SENATOR IN 1992; SHE WAS RE-ELECTED TO A THIRD SENATE TERM IN 2004.

g a ★ Difference

There is no greater legacy to the suffrage movement in Washington than the women who made a difference in their own time and place. The women featured here are among countless others who, by building a better future, honored those who came before them.

Mother Joseph
A Sister of Providence (1823–1902)

Mother Joseph often signed her letters, "your humble daughter," but there was nothing humble about her accomplishments. The French-Canadian nun arrived in the Pacific Northwest in 1856 to find the place was devoid of schools and hospitals. An architect and carpenter, Mother Joseph (Esther Pariseau) opened the region's first hospital in Vancouver, Washington, in 1858. Over the next 40 years she led construction of 30 hospitals, schools, and orphanages throughout the Pacific Northwest. She is one of two Washingtonians representing the state in National Statuary Hall, Washington, D.C.

Nettie J. Asberry

Activist and NAACP Founder (1865–1968)

A stalwart club member, Nettie Asberry cultivated change through the Tacoma Cloverleaf Club and as a charter member of the Washington Federation of Colored Women's Clubs. In 1913, when the Washington legislature attempted to outlaw interracial marriage, Nettie Asberry led protests to kill the bill. It died in committee. As founder of the Tacoma NAACP, Asberry fought racial segregation in public places and at Fort Lewis—at a time when it was dangerous to do so. Thought to be one of the first African American women to earn a doctorate degree (in music), she taught piano to Tacoma's children for nearly a half century.

Julia Butler Hansen

Democratic Congresswoman (1907–1988)

A s state legislator from Cathlamet from 1939 to 1960, Julia Butler Hansen served on or chaired the house highway committee for nearly two decades, leading efforts to construct Interstate-5 and many other highways. She served seven terms in the U. S. House of Representatives, ending in 1974, and was the first woman to chair a House appropriations subcommittee. "No one represented her people better than (Hansen)," said long-time Washington senator Warren Magnuson.

Lucy Friedlander Covington

Colville Confederated Tribes Leader (1910–1982)

Lucy Covington was born November 24, 1910, north of Nespelem, in a teepee. Her ancestors included Chief Kamiakin of the Yakima tribe and Chief Owayi of the Nez Perce. Chief Moses was her great-grandfather. As an advocate and leader in the Colville Confederated Tribes, Covington battled to prevent the federal government from closing the Colville Reservation in the 1960s. Often at odds with other tribal leaders who wanted to sell the land, Covington believed it would spell the end of Colville Indian culture. Her grandmother, Mary Moses, deeply ingrained in her the idea: "Take land before you ever take money. If you have land, you have identity." She was the first woman to serve as tribal council chair of the Confederated Tribes and had a 24-year tenure on the council.

Ruby Chow

County Councilwoman, Activist (1920–2008)

Ruby Chow was the first Asian American woman elected to the King County Council, but her greatest contribution was bringing cultures together. As owner of Seattle's first upscale Chinese restaurant—Ruby Chow's—she introduced Seattle to Chinese cuisine and culture. The popularity of Asian food in the Northwest started at Ruby Chow's in the 1960s. Chow became a tireless activist for the people of Chinatown and served four terms on the county council.

Jennifer Dunn

Republican Congresswoman (1941–2007)

Jennifer Dunn leaped the gender gap in Republican Party politics. She was the first woman to lead the Washington State Republican Party, and also served as its chairwoman. In 1992 she was elected to the first of her six terms in Congress, representing the Seattle and Bellevue areas. She was the first freshman woman to earn a place on the House Republican leadership team and won a prized seat on the Ways and Means Committee. One colleague said of her, "Jennifer Dunn really had a 'W' after her name because she worked tirelessly for Washington and put its best interests above partisan interests."

Dora Sánchez-Treviño

Anti-violence Activist

Dora Sánchez-Treviño sat at her son's deathbed and made a promise. Seventeen-year-old Auggie, murdered by a gang member in 1999, would not die in vain. She vowed she would spend the rest of her life raising public awareness of the toll violence takes on children and communities. Treviño, founder of Stop the Violence in Our Communities and the first Latina city councilwoman in Quincy, speaks frequently in schools around the nation, teaching students how to avoid violence.

Dr. Bonnie Dunbar

Astronaut

D r. Bonnie Dunbar's impact goes beyond state and country—it reaches into space. One of NASA's first female astronauts and a Washington native, Dunbar is a veteran of five shuttle missions. In her last mission she was payload commander, responsible for four tons of materials and equipment being delivered to the Russian space station, Mir. Dunbar is currently president and CEO of Seattle's Museum of Flight.

Appendix A

REFORM LEGISLATION AFTER WOMEN'S SUFFRAGE[342]

1911

Women did not vote for this legislature as the members ran concurrently with the suffrage proposition.

Eight-hour law for all women workers except fish and fruit industries.

"Seats for Employees" law strengthened by adding the provision that copy of law must be posted in all establishments subject to it.

Service of women on jury made optional (two-thirds of women serve when called).

1913

Legislature, except half the senate, voted for by women. (First women in legislature are Nena Jolidon Croake and Francis Axtell.) Josephine Corliss Preston serves as first woman superintendent of public instruction.

Mothers' pension law—benefits to married women abandoned for one year as well as to women whose husbands are disabled, insane, or in penal institutions. For the benefit of children under 15 years. Monthly allowance is $15 for one child, $5 for each additional child.

Repeal of the corroborative evidence law in sexual assault cases. (Representative Frances H. Axtell and Ella Higginson were proponents of this change.)

Minimum wage law—Industrial Welfare Commission fixes "minimum wage" for women "adequate for maintenance" and for minors "suitable."

Red light abatement law—fine and sale of personal property.

Abolition of capital punishment.

"Lazy Husband Law"—if the husband is able to work, he is forced to work for county and $1.50 per day paid to wife.

Juvenile court law.

Protection of incompetents, children, and animals.

Formation of the Industrial Welfare Commission to study, recommend, and enforce a minimum wage for women.

1914

By initiative and referendum, statewide prohibition goes into effect January 1916. The vote carried 190,000 to 171,000

1915

Legislature first voted for as a whole by women.

Mothers' pension law amended to deprive divorced mothers of its benefits.

1916

Attempt to repeal liquor laws defeated.

Measures related to initiative, referendum, and recall; against municipal ownership; and anti-picketing laws defeated.

1917

Bone-dry prohibition.

Single standard for adultery.

Teachers' retirement fund.

Defeat of 10-hour candy makers' bill.

Defeat of restoration of capital punishment.

Vocational training.

1918

Bone-dry law passed.

1919

Ratification of national prohibition amendment.

Child maintenance law. Amendment of mothers' pension law to remove all restrictions except motherhood, necessity, and residence. Under this law both divorced and unmarried mothers receive benefits.

Equal pay for men and women teachers.

Midwifery law. Examination and certification.

Single standard for age of consent (18 years old).

Women's Industrial Home and Clinic.

Unmarried mother's law making the adjudicated father of the child of an unmarried mother responsible for child maintenance until 16 years.

Laws to prevent the spread of venereal disease.

Anti-cigarette law.

Compulsory physical training.

Vocational training. Part-time schools for workers between 14 and 18—four hours per week during school term.

Teachers' retirement fund amendment.

1920

Special session to ratify the women's suffrage amendment to u.s. Constitution.

Appendix B

MODERN WASHINGTON WOMEN'S EQUAL RIGHTS SUMMARY CHRONOLOGY[343]

CATHERINE MAY, WASHINGTON'S FIRST ELECTED CONGRESSWOMAN.

1959   Catherine May is the first woman elected to Congress from Washington.

1963   Washington Legislature formally repeals the prohibition on women holding public office.

1963   Washington Governor Rosellini appoints a 29-member Commission on the Status of Women in Washington.

1968   Governor Dan Evans reconstitutes the Commission on the Status of Women in Washington.

1970   Washington voters approve Referendum 20, which legalized abortion in early pregnancy. The measure passed by 4,222 votes out of 1,509, 402 votes cast.

1970   Governor Dan Evans creates the Interagency Advisory Committee on the Status of Women with instructions to determine how many recommendations of the Commission on the Status of Women had been carried out.

1971   Sex is added to the employment section of the Washington State Law Against Discrimination (RCW 49.60) HB 594.

1971   Women can sue for personal injuries in their own name and manage their own salaries.

1971   A reconstituted Washington State Women's Council is appointed by Governor Dan Evans. This was a recommendation of the Interagency Advisory Committee on the Status of Women.

1972   League of Women Voters, "Status of Women in Washington State" is published.

1972   Washington State Voters ratify an Equal Rights Amendment to the Washington State Constitution.

1972   Washington legislature passes a community property measure that requires that ownership and management of assets be equally shared between married partners.

1972   Washington legislature passes a law allowing a married woman to sue for personal injury in her own name.

1972   Washington legislature passes legislation so that women can have their own credit rating separate from that of their husbands.

1973   March 22, 1973, Washington legislature ratifies the Equal Rights Amendment to the Constitution of the United States.

1973   Washington legislature passes "no fault" divorce.

1973   HB 404 expanded Washington State Law Against Discrimination by adding "sex" and "marital status" to the existing categories of employment, real estate, insurance and credit.

1973   New categories are added to Washington State Job Classifications to bridge the gap between clerical and professional positions, the first in the nation.

1973   Creation of the "Roster of Qualified Women" by the Washington Women's Council which created a pool of women for gubernatorial appointments to Boards.

1974   Study on Comparable Worth completed and submitted to Governor Dan Evans.

1975   Washington bans sex discrimination in textbooks and audio visual materials for public school teachers and students.

1975   State Personnel Office changes procedures to recognize volunteer service as work experience on state job applications.

1975   Washington legislature passes a revised Rape Law.

1975   Governor reconstitutes Washington State Women's Council.

1976   The Tax Reform Act of 1976 allows tax credits for child care.

1976   Dixie Lee Ray is elected Washington's first woman governor.

1976   Phase II of Comparable Worth study completed. Study reveals that overall, women were receiving 20% lower pay than men for comparable work.

1976   Changes in policy of leasing public lands—organizations that did not allow women could not lease lands.

1976   Dual listing of the names of both husbands and wives in telephone books adopted by Washington State Utilities and Transportation Commission.

1977   Washington State Apprenticeship Council includes women in affirmative action plans.

1977   Washington State Women's Commission legislation is passed by the Legislature creating a cabinet level organization.

1977   Publication of "Women and the Law in Washington State" legal handbook.

1977   Displaced Homemaker Law.

1977   Victims of Sexual Assault Bill.

1977   Washington State Creditors must report credit to reflect participation of both spouses.

1977   July—Washington State Conference for Women in Ellensburg part of the state's participation in International Women's Year.

1977   November—Referendum 40 passed in Washington which was a vote against the creation of the Washington State Women's Commission.

1978   Governor Dixie Lee Ray determines in April that the Women's Council would be phased out by September 1, 1978.

1983   Washington State Comparable Worth Lawsuit in Federal Court.

1983–84 Salary adjustment reflecting Comparable Worth be included in salary survey package. Required it be achieved by 1993.

1985   Ninth Circuit Court of Appeals reverses lower Washington Court decision on Comparable Worth.

1985   Legislature appropriates additional funds for comparable worth and negotiations between the state and WFSE. Settlement is reached on December 1985.

1986   Comparable worth agreement between Washington State and WFSE ratified in 1986 by the state legislature. The $482 million settlement benefited 34,000 state employees.

1991   Initiative 120 is approved which repealed the former abortion rights initiative and replaced it with one that declares that "every individual possesses a fundamental right of privacy with respect to personal reproductive decisions" (RCW, Chapter 9.02, Initiative Measure No. 120 1991).

1992   The Washington legislature sets a national record with the highest proportion of elected female lawmakers of any state in the country.

1999   The Washington legislature sets a national record with 41 percent elected women lawmakers.

2003   When Justice Mary E. Fairhurst was sworn into office on January 13, it was the first time in Washington State history that the Supreme Court had a female majority.

2004   Washington's Second Woman Governor, Chris Gregoire is elected.

2005   Washington became the first state to have, at the same time, a woman governor (Chris Gregoire) and two women U.S. Senators (Patty Murray and Maria Cantwell).

2005   Women's History Consortium established under the auspices of the Washington State Historical Society.

2008   Chris Gregoire reelected as governor.

Appendix 6

WOMEN IN ELECTIVE OFFICE

U.S. Congress[344]

Maria Cantwell (D), U.S. Senator, 2001–present

Patty Murray (D), U.S. Senator, 1993–present

Cathy McMorris Rogers (R), U.S. Rep., 2005–present

Jennifer Dunn (R), U.S. Rep., 1993–2005

Linda Ann Smith (R), U.S. Rep., 1995–1999

Maria Cantwell (D), U.S. Rep., 1993–1995

Jolene Unsoeld (D), U.S. Rep., 1989–1995

Julia Butler Hansen (D), U.S. Rep. 1960–1974
(*Hansen won a special election to fill a vacancy caused by death. She was subsequently reelected.*)

Catherine D. May (R), U.S. Rep., 1959–1971

Statewide Elective Executives[345]

Christine O. Gregoire (D), Governor, 2005–present; Attorney General, 1993–2005

Theresa Bergeson (NP), Superintendent of Public Instruction, 1997–2008

Jennifer Belcher (D), Commissioner of Public Lands, 1993–2001

Deborah Senn (D), Commissioner of Insurance, 1993–2001

Judith Billings (NP), Superintendent of Public Instruction, 1989–1997

Dixy Lee Ray (D), Governor, 1977–1981

Pearl A. Wanamaker (NP), Superintendent of Public Instruction, 1941–1956

Belle C. Reeves (D), Secretary of State, 1939–1948

Josephine C. Preston (NP), Superintendent of Public Instruction, 1913–1928

Women on the Washington State Supreme Court

Carolyn R. Dimmick, 1981–1985

Barbara Durham, 1985–2000

Barbara Madsen, 1993–present

Roselle Pekelis, 1995–1996

Faith Ireland, 1999–2005

Bobbe J. Bridge, 2000–2008

Susan J. Owens, 2001–present

Mary E. Fairhurst, 2003–present

Debra L. Stephens, 2008–present

Notes

1. Merriam-Webster's Collegiate Dictionary, 10th ed., s.v. "suffrage."

2. Abigail Adams to John Adams, March 31, 1776, http://www.thelizlibrary.org/suffrage/abigail.htm. Historically, the term used for the right for women to vote was *woman suffrage*. The contemporary usage—*women's suffrage*—is employed throughout the book.

3. For more on the convention's organization and attendees, see Judith Wellman, *The Road to Seneca Falls: Elizabeth Cady Stanton and the First Woman's Rights Convention* (Urbana: University of Illinois Press, 2004).

4. Wellman, 193.

5. Women's Rights National Historical Park, "Declaration of Sentiments" and "Report of the Women's Rights Convention," http://www.nps.gov/wori/historyculture/report-of-the-womans-rights-convention.htm.

6. Ibid.

7. Fourteenth Amendment, http://www.usconstitution.net/xconst_Am14.html.

8. Fifteenth Amendment, http://www.historicaldocuments.com/15thAmendment.htm. Ellen Carol Dubois, "Taking the Law into Our Own Hands," in *One Woman, One Vote: Rediscovering the Woman Suffrage Movement* e, ed. Marjorie Spruill Wheeler (Troutdale, OR: New Sage Press, 1996), 84.

9. After Washington were California, 1911; Oregon, Kansas, and Arizona, 1912; Montana and Nevada 1914; New York, 1917, Michigan, South Dakota, and Oklahoma, 1918. Other states enacted presidential or primary suffrage during this time. National American Woman Suffrage Association, *Victory: How Women Won It: A Centennial Symposium* (New York: H. W Wilson Company, 1940), 161-164.

10. See Sylvia Van Kirk, *Many Tender Ties: Women in the Fur-Trade Society, 1670-1870* (Norman: University of Oklahoma, 1983).

11. New York passed the first Married Women's Property Act in 1848.

12. Richard H. Chused, "The Oregon Donation Act of 1850 and Nineteenth-Century Federal Married Women's Property Law," *Law and History Review* 2 (Spring 1984): 44-78, esp. 44.

13. Washington Territorial Legislature, *Journal of the House, Territory of Washington*, 1st sess., (Olympia, 1854), 98.

14. Washington Territorial Legislature, *Journal of the Council, Territory of Washington*, 1st sess., (Olympia, 1854), 58-61; and Stella E. Pierce, "Suffrage in the Pacific Northwest: Old Oregon and Washington," *Washington Historical Quarterly* 3 (April 1912): 106-14, esp. 109.

15. Clyde B. Simmons, "The History of Woman Suffrage in the State of Washington" (master's thesis, University of Washington, 1903), 3.

16. Washington Territorial Legislature, *Laws of Washington Territory* (Olympia, 1867), 5.

17. See Richard A. Seiber, ed., *Memoirs of Puget Sound: Early Seattle 1853-1856, The Letters of David & Catherine [sic] Blaine* (Fairfield, Wash.: Ye Galleon Press, 1978); and "Register of Voters," *Seattle Post-Intelligencer*, July 12, 1885, 4.

18. T. Alfred Larson, "The Woman Suffrage Movement in Washington," *Pacific Northwest Quarterly* 67, no. 2 (April 1976): 49-62, quotation on 49.

19. Elizabeth Cady Stanton, Susan B. Anthony, Matilda Joslyn Gage, and Ida Husted Harper, eds., *History of Woman Suffrage*, 6 vols. (Rochester: J. J. Little & Co., 1881-1922), 3:784. Hereafter cited *HWS*.

20. Ibid.

21. Stanton and others, "Mrs. Brown's Argument," in *HWS* 3: 784-85

22. "Results of Election," *Olympia Transcript*, June 11, 1870, 2.

23. Rebecca Mead, *How the Vote Was Won*, (New York: New York University Press, 2004), 37. Dubois, "Taking the Law into Our Own Hands," 81-98.

24. Dubois, "Taking the Law into Our Own Hands," 84-85.

25. Doug Linder, "The Trial of Susan B. Anthony for Illegal Voting," University of Missouri-Kansas City School of Law, http://www.law.umkc.edu/faculty/projects/ftrials/anthony/sbaaccount.html.

26. Other important cases were *Bradwell v. Illinois*, 18 U.S. 130 (1873); *Slaughterhouse Cases*, 83 U.S. 36 (1873); as well as *Minor v. Happersett*, 88 U.S. 162 (1875), and Mead, *How the Vote Was Won*, 37.

27. Dubois, "Taking the Law into Our Own Hands," 97.

28. See Nelson A. Ault, "The Earnest Ladies: The Walla Walla Woman's Club and the Equal Suffrage League of 1886-1889," *Pacific Northwest Quarterly* 42 (1951): 123-37, for more information on the Isaacs and other Walla Walla suffragists.

29. G. Thomas Edwards, *Sowing Good Seeds: The Northwest Suffrage Campaigns of Susan B. Anthony* (Portland: Oregon Historical Society Press, 1990); *Walla Walla Statesman*, September 30; and *Walla Walla Statesman*, October 7, 1871. See also Susan B. Anthony Papers (Library of Congress, Wash., D.C.), Daybook and Diaries 1856–1906, Box 2 Reel 1–2, for her diary from September 18 to 25, 1871, and October 16–November 11, 1871.

30. Edwards, *Sowing Good Seeds*, 86.

31. Edwards, *Sowing Good Seeds*, 88. This is likely untrue, but stated by Anthony.

32 "Miss Anthony's Speech," *Olympia Transcript*, October 21, 1871.

33 "Woman Suffrage," *Washington Standard*, October 21, 1871.

34 Edwards, *Sowing Good Seeds*, 87-92.

35 Ibid., 97.

36 Ibid., 101.

37 "Afternoon Session," *Washington Standard*, November 11, 1871.

38 Officers were J. B. Allen; Annie Mix (Walla Walla), L. Ellen Hewitt (Olympia), Sarah B. Yesler (Seattle), Mrs. Amelia Giddings (Olympia), Lizzie Ordway (Port Madison), and E. T. Munson (Olympia). Serving on the Finance Committee were John M. Murphy, Mary Ann Barnes, Albert. A. Manning—all from Olympia. The Executive Committee included Olympia residents Ann Elizabeth White Bigelow, Mary Olney Brown, Mehitable Elder, Phoebe Moore, Mary Saunders, Clara Sylvester, and Sara L. Theobalds (Seattle), Caroline M. Willis (White River), and Mary E. Meigs (Port Madison).

39 "Woman Suffrage Convention," *Washington Standard*, November 11, 1871, 2; and Simmons, "History of Woman Suffrage in the State of Washington," 22. Anti-suffragists were James H. Lasater of Walla Walla and Mrs. J. B. Frost, and pro-suffragists were Father (likely A. A.) Denny, Alfred Elder, John Denny, and Abigail Scott Duniway.

40 Edwards, *Sowing Good Seeds*, 109-110.

41 See Abigail Scott Duniway, *Path Breaking*, (Portland, Oregon: James, Kerns & Abbot Co., 1914); Ruth Barnes Moynihan, *Rebel for Rights: Abigail Scott Duniway* (New Haven: Yale University Press, 1983); Dorothy Nafus Morrison, *Ladies Were Not Expected: Abigail Scott Duniway and Women's Rights* (New York: Atheneum, 1977).

42 Chused, "The Oregon Donation Act of 1850," 44.

43 Thomas R. Andrews and others, eds., *Washington Community Property Deskbook* (Washington State Bar Association 2003), 1-1.

44 Statue Law Committee, *Revised Code of Washington*, sec. 26.16.030 (OLYMPIA, 2008).

45 The Territory of Puerto Rico also has community property laws.

46 Pierce, *Suffrage in the Pacific Northwest*, 109. Washington Territorial Legislature, *Statutes of Washington Territory* (Olympia, 1855), 325; *Acts of the Legislative Assembly* (Olympia, 1858), 22; *Statutes of Washington Territory* (Olympia, 1863), 470; *Statutes of Washington Territory* (Olympia, 1866), 18; *Statutes of Washington Territory* (Olympia, 1871), 27-28; *Laws of Washington Territory* (Olympia, 1877), 268.

47 Pierce, "Suffrage in the Pacific Northwest," 109.

48 Washington Territorial Legislature, *Statutes of Washington Territory* (Olympia, 1871), 435.

49 Washington Territorial Legislature, *Laws of Washington Territory* (Olympia, 1877), 268.

50 Ibid.

51 Larson, "Woman Suffrage Movement in Washington," 52.

52 Mead, *How the Vote Was Won*, 4-6.

53 Mary Olney Brown, "Mrs. Brown Attempts to Vote," in *HWS* 3: 787.

54 "Washington's First Constitution, 1878," *Washington Historical Quarterly* 9 (April, 1918): 129-52, esp. 137.

55 Ibid., 138.

56 Separate Article #1: "No person, otherwise a qualified voter, shall be denied the right to vote on account of sex, anything in this constitution to the contrary notwithstanding." Vote was 1,827 for and 5,117 against. Separate Article #2: "No person shall be denied the right, on account of sex, to vote or hold office in this state; nor shall such right be, in any manner, abridged on account of sex." Vote was 1,745 for and 5,061 against. Washington State Archives records, Olympia.

57 "Washington's First Constitution, 1878," 139-40.

58 Simmons, "History of Woman Suffrage in the State of Washington," 24.

59 "Be it enacted by the Legislature of the Territory of Washington: Sec. 1. All female citizens of the age of 21 years shall be entitled to vote at all elections in the territory, subject only to such regulations as male citizens. Sec. 2. Any officer of election who shall refuse to take the vote of a woman citizen (otherwise qualified to vote), shall be liable to a fine of not less than $100 nor more than $500. Sec. 3. All laws in conflict with this act are hereby repealed. Sec. 4. This act to be in force on and after its passage." Simmons, "History of Woman Suffrage in the State of Washington," 24.

60 William H. White (aka "Warhorse Bill") was a prominent Washington jurist. He served in several capacities, including prosecuting attorney, legislator from King County, U.S. attorney, and Washington State Supreme Court Justice. In 1912 he helped his wife, Emma McRedmond White, in her bid for King County clerk. She also organized the Woman's Democratic Club in King County. Georgeann Malowney, "Justice William Henry White," redmondwashington.org, http://www.redmondwashington.org/biography/white/white-william-henry.htm.

61 Mary Olney Brown, "Introduction of a Suffrage Bill," in *HWS* 3: 787.

62 Washington Territorial Legislature, *Code of Washington Territory, Chapter CLXXXIII, Property Rights of Married Persons* (Olympia, 1881), 413-416; and Simmons, "History of Woman Suffrage," 25-26.

63 Sandra F. Van Burkleo, "'A Double-Head in Nature Is a Monstrosity': Re-Covering the Married Woman

in Frontier Washington, 1879-1892" (paper, Annual Meeting of the American Society for Legal History, Seattle, Wash., October 21-24, 1998), 12.

64 Larson, "Woman Suffrage Movement in Washington," 52.

65 Ibid., 53; and Mead, 46, 98.

66 Duniway, "Passage of Suffrage Bill," in *HWS* 3: 777.

67 Larson, "Woman Suffrage Movement in Washington," 53; and C. B. Bagley, "Women Lobbyists," *Puget Sound Weekly Courier*, November 13, 1883.

68 The bill was introduced in the house or representatives by Representative Copley, and was supported in speeches by Messrs. Copley, Besserer, Miles, Clark, and Stitzel, while Messrs. Landrum and Kincaid spoke against it. The vote was: Ayes—Besserer, Brooks, Clark, Copley, Foster, Goodell, Hungate, Kuhn, Lloyd, Martin Miles, Shaw, Stitzel, and Speaker Ferguson—14. Noes—Barlow, Brining, Landrum, Pin, Kincaid, Shoudy, and Young—7. Absent—Blackwell, Turpin, and Warner—3. The bill was favorably reported in the council, November 15, by Chairman Burk of the Judiciary Committee. No one offered to speak on it. The vote stood: Ayes—Burk, Edmiston, Hale, Harper, Kerr, Power, and Smith—7. Noes—Caton, Collins, Houghton, Whitehouse, and President Ruax—5. Governor W. A. Newell approved the bill November 22, 1883.

69 Duniway, "Passage of Suffrage Bill," in *HWS* 3: 777.

70 Larson, "Woman Suffrage Movement in Washington," 53.

71 Mead, 47.

72 Quoted in, "Afternoon Session," *Washington Standard*, October 19, 1883, 2. See also Mead, *How the Vote Was Won*, 47.

73 Larson, "Woman Suffrage Movement in Washington," 53.

74 Abigail Scott Duniway, "The Ratification," *The New Northwest*, November 22, 1883.

75 Mead, *How the Vote Was Won*, 99.

76 Sandra Haarsager, *Organized Womanhood: Cultural Politics in the Pacific Northwest, 1840-1920* (Norman: University of Oklahoma, 1997), 10.

77 Karen J. Blair, *The Clubwoman as Feminist: True Womanhood Redefined, 1868-1914* (New York: Holmes & Meier Publishers, 1988), 70; and Dr. Karen J. Blair, e-mail to author, December 30, 2008.

78 These women formed the Columbia Maternal Association to discuss topics associated with motherhood—the first club of women in Washington. See Clifford Drury, "The Columbia Maternal Association," *Oregon Historical Quarterly* 39 (June 1938): 99-122.

79 From Clinton A Snowden, *History of Washington: The Rise and Progress of an American State* (New York: Century History, 1909), 113-14. Members listed are Gay Hayden, Mrs. M. E. Nicholson, Mrs. Amanda Loomis, Mrs.

Caroline Whitney, Mrs. Mary Turnbull, Mrs. Susan Turnbull, Mrs. S. A. Fletcher, Mrs. Sarah Hakes, Mrs. E. S. McConnell, Mrs. Elizabeth Durgin, Mrs. Middleton, Mrs. Laura Slocum, Mrs. R. Brown, Mrs. Eliza Troupe, Mrs. Freeman, and Mrs. M. S. Stablet.

80 Mead, *How the Vote Was Won*, 99.

81 Abigail Scott Duniway, *Path Breaking* (Portland: James, Kerns and Abbott Co., 1914), 206-207.

82 Haarsager, *Organized Womanhood*, 274-275.

83 Putnam, "A 'Test of Chiffon Politics,'" 613.

84 Dr. Karen J. Blair, "The History of Women's Clubs" (Washington State History Museum, Tacoma, 29 March 2007), http://www.washingtonwomenshistory.org/themes/clubs/historyOfClubsBlairAudio.aspx.

85 Esther Mumford e-mail message and telephone call to the author, January 2009.

86 Mead, *How the Vote Was Won*, 47.

87 Martha E. Pike, "Washington," in *HWS* 4: 967.

88 "Open Air Convention," *Seattle Daily Post Intelligencer*, June 14, 1884; and Dorothy Brant Brazier, "Women's Lib Nothing New, *Seattle Times*, n.d.

89 "Washington," *Women's Journal*, in *HWS* 4: 1096.

90 Ibid.

91 Cornelia Jenner to Mrs. Foster, July 14, 1884, clipping provided by Kathryn Crossley.

92 Charles K. Wiggins, "Charles S. Voorhees and the Omnibus Admissions Act," 1989, Wiggins & Masters, http://www.appeal-law.com/constitution/voorhees.html.

93 Other cases in which women's roles as jurors were challenged and upheld include *George Schilling v. Territory of Washington*, 2 Wash. Terr. 283 (1884); *Walker v. Territory of Washington*, 2 Wash. Terr. 186 5P. 313 (1884); *Hays v. Territory of Washington*, 2 Wash. Terr. 286, 5P. 927 (1884).

94 Claudius O. Johnson, "George Turner, Part I: The Background of a Statesman," *Pacific Northwest Quarterly* 34 (July 1943): 243-69; "George Turner, Part II: United States Senator and Counsel and Arbiter for the United States," *Pacific Northwest Quarterly* 34 (July 1943): 367-92.

95 *Rosencrantz v. Territory of Washington*, 2 Wash. Terr. 267 (1884).

96 Murray Morgan, "Washington Women's Roller Coaster Ride to the Franchise," in *Pacific Northwest: Essays in Honor of James W. Scott*, ed. Howard J. Critchfield (Bellingham: Western Washington University Press, 1993), 113.

97 Washington Territorial Legislature, *Laws of Washington Territory* (Olympia, 1886), 113-114.

98 Morgan, "Washington Women's Roller Coaster Ride," 112; and Morgan, "Harry Morgan and His Business," Tacoma Public Library, http://www2.tacomapubliclibrary.org/v2/NWRoom/MORGAN/Morgan.htm.

99 *Harland v. Territory of Washington*, 3 Wash. Terr. 131 (1887).

100 "Woman Suffrage Dissatisfaction with the Recent Decision in Washington Territory from the *Portland Oregonian*," *New York Times*, February 21, 1887, 5.

101 The women included Mary E. Kentworthy, Nellie Wood, Mary Scott, Fannie Smith, Carrie Jones, Adaline Weed, Carrie Hill, Florence Chick, and Elizabeth Mooers.

102 "The Woman's Meeting," *Seattle Daily Post-Intelligencer*, February 10, 1887, 3.

103 "That Indignation Meeting," *Seattle Daily Post-Intelligencer*, March 3, 1887, 3.

104 Mead, *How the Vote Was Won*, 6, 7.

105 Alan Hynding, *The Public Life of Eugene Semple, Promoter and Politician of the Northwest* (Seattle: University of Washington Press, 1973), 78-81.

106 John Fahey, "The Nevada Bloomer Case," *Columbia* 2, no. 2 (Summer 1988): 42-45; and "Washington Appendix," in *HWS* 4: 1098.

107 *Bloomer v. Todd*, 3 Wash. Terr. 599 (1888).

108 Fahey, "Nevada Bloomer Case," 45; and Adella Parker, "How Washington Women Lost the Ballot," in *Washington Women's Cook Book* (Seattle: Trade Register Print, 1909), 204-209, esp. 207.

109 Mead, *How the Vote Was Won*, 49.

110 Bagley, *History of Seattle* (Seattle: S. J. Clark Publishing Co., 1916), 2:489. Labor and anti-Chinese activists rounded up Chinese residents in Seattle and forced them to the docks to leave on a steamer. Governor Watson C. Squire prevented the ship from leaving but more than two hundred Chinese left for San Francisco. After mob violence, martial law was declared by Governor Squire and President Cleveland. Walt Crowley, "Anti-Chinese Activism in Seattle," May 2, 1999, HistoryLink, http://www.historylink.org/essays/output.cfm?file_id=1057.

111 Mead, *How the Vote Was Won*, 41.

112 Priscilla Long, "Tacoma Expels the Entire Chinese Community on November 3, 1885," January 17, 2003, HistoryLink, http://www.historylink.org/essays/output.cfm?file_id=5063; Crowley, "Anti-Chinese Activism in Seattle"; and Mead, *How the Vote Was Won*, 40.

113 Parker, "How Washington Women Lost the Ballot," 207.

114 Gary L. Geiger, "Adele Parker: The Case Study of a Woman in the Progressive Era" (master's thesis, Western Washington University, 1979). King County teacher, lawyer, suffragist, and political activist, Parker served as WESA press agent during the 1909-1910 campaign. She was Washington's representative on the National Executive Committee of NAWSA and President of the College Equal Suffrage League of King County. Parker also acted as assistant editor of *Votes for Women*, and following the suffrage victory in Washington, she began a regional publication titled *Western Woman Voter*. In 1934, she served as a member of the Washington State House of Representatives. Her long career as a political activist included a stint with the American Civil Liberties Union (ACLU). She opened the first ACLU office in Seattle and for some time was its lone employee. Her work for the ACLU included efforts to free the IWW workers imprisoned after the Centralia Massacre. (Compiled from Washington Women's History Consortium sources.)

115 *Thornton v. Territory of Washington*, 3 Wash. Terr. 48. (1888).

116 Parker, "How Washington Women Lost the Ballot," 207.

117 Mead, *How the Vote was Won*, 49. Zerelda McCoy of Tacoma, national vice-president of the Woman's Suffrage Association, along with Elizabeth McIntosh of Seattle and Barbara Thompson of Tacoma, served as the Washington Territory leaders of the Equal Suffrage League, established in March 1889.

118 Beverly Paulik Rosenow, ed., *The Journal of the Washington State Constitutional Convention* (1889; rpt. Seattle: Book Publishing Company, 1962), 642-43. Petitioners: P.G. Hendricks, 394 other men and 414 women; William West and others; Francis Miner of St. Louis; A. M. Sweeney, Jennie Aukney, and others of Walla Walla; H. J. Beeks and others; Mr. Giliam and others; Marty T. Jones and others; G. C. Barron and others; W. V. Anders and others; Lucinda King and others; L. W. Studgall and others; W. P. Stewart and others; P. J. Flint and others; Zerelda McCoy and 26 teachers; Dr. A. K. Bush and 94 others; S. M. Ballard and 151 others; George E. Cline and 163 others; L. M. Lord and 82 others; C. F. Woodcock and 120 others; 93 voters of Buckley; and Zerelda McCoy, a taxpaying woman.

119 Charles K. Wiggins, "John P. Hoyt & Women Suffrage," 1988, Wiggins & Masters, http://www.c-wiggins.com/constitution/hoyt.html.

120 "The Woman Suffragists: Attempt to Turn Their Big Gun Loose on the Convention," *Tacoma Morning Globe*, July 24, 1889, 1, cols. 1-3.

121 Wiggins, "Hoyt & Women Suffrage."

122 Clara Bewick Colby, accounts from *The Woman's Tribune*, April 1–June 29, 1889. "Far-Off Sounds, Number I," April 20, 1889; "Far-Off Sounds, Number II," May 4, 1889; "Far-Off Sounds, Number IV," May 11, 1889; "Far-Off Sounds, Number V," May 18, 1889, "Far-Off Sounds, Number V—Spokane Falls," May 25, 1889; "Far-Off Sounds, Number VI," June 1, 1889; "Far-Off Sounds, Number VII," June 15, 1889; "Far-Off Sounds, Number VIII," June 29, 1889. Colby traveled to Whatcom County where she worked with Mrs. Saxon, Mrs. C. M. Kellogg, and May Van Auken. She journeyed on to Wollochet Bay and Puyallup where she consulted with Elizabeth Palmer Spinning and Eliza

Jane Meeker. She proceeded to Buckley and then to Olympia where she met with Abbie H. H. Stuart and arranged for noted California suffragist Laura de Force Gordon to speak at the Opera House there. Colby then went to Tacoma to work with Zerelda McCoy to arrange Gordon's presentations in Tacoma.. Colby soldiered on to Ellensburg, arranging lectures there and in Roslyn and Cleaburn. She went on to North Yakima and helped organize a Pasco suffrage society of twenty-five members. She was greeted in Spokane Falls where she arranged for several lectures by Gordon and worked with the Spokane Suffrage Association whose president was Robert Abernethy. Colby pointedly stated that Spokane was the home of anti-suffragists Judge George Turner, Judge Nash, and Nevada Bloomer. It was then on to Sprague, Ritzville, and Wallula to meet with other suffrage groups. Colby worked extensively with ministers (often Methodists) and local WCTU members in organizing the territory for women's rights. Colby traveled next to Walla Walla, where she noted there was an established suffrage association, with Lucie Isaacs as president. She connected with suffragists in Garfield, Colfax, Pomeroy, Riparaia, Dayton, and Waitsburg. Returning to the Puget Sound area, she visited with the Palmers, Clara D. Peterson, and. Mrs. K A. Webster in establishing an organization in Steilacoom. She went to Snohomish and there met with Asa Mercer in Seattle helping to organize suffrage groups in those locales as well as in Centralia, Kelso, and Castle Rock.

123 "Washington, Appendix," in HWS 4: 1098.

124 Clara Bewick Colby, "To Suffrage Societies of Washington," The Woman's Tribune, September 21, 1889.

125 Ault, "Earnest Ladies," 135-36.

126 Van Burkleo, "'A Double-Head in Nature Is a Monstrosity,'" 56.

127 Parker, "How Washington Women Lost the Ballot," 207, 208

128 Washington State Legislature, Washington State Session Laws (Olympia, 1889-90), 377.

129 Washington State Legislature, Washington State Session Laws (Olympia, 1895), 66.

130 Martha E. Pike, "Washington," in HWS 4: 978-79; and Mildred Andrews, "Women Win School Suffrage, March 27, 1890," HistoryLink, http://www.historylink.org/essays/printer_friendly/index.cfm?file_id=469.

131 Dr. Karen Blair, e-mail message to author, September 4, 2008.

132 Lucile McDonald, "The Battle over the State Flower," Seattle Times Magazine, January 31, 1965, 2, Museum of History and Industry, Seattle; Ruth Fry Epperson, "Rhododendron…," unpublished MS, 1964, #3359, MOHAI, Seattle.

133 Aaron Caplan, "The History of Women's Jury Service in Washington," Washington State Bar News, March 2005, 12-21.

134 Martha E. Pike "Washington," in HWS 4: 975. Upon the death of Edward Eldridge in 1892, Olympia resident and Woman's Club of Olympia founder Abbie H. H. Stuart took over the presidency of the state suffrage association. Laura Peters was vice-president, and Bessie Isaacs Savage was secretary. In 1895, the Washington State Suffrage Association held the first "delegate" convention in Olympia. Delegates elected Savage president; Clara Sylvester vice-president; Lou Jackson Longmire secretary; and Ella Stork treasurer.

135 See T. Alfred Larson, "Woman's Rights in Idaho," Idaho Yesterdays 16 (Spring 1971): 2-15; and Larson, "Woman Suffrage in Wyoming," Pacific Northwest Quarterly 56 (April 1965): 57-66.

136 The added language was that "they shall be able to read and speak the English language . . . . The legislature shall enact laws defining the manner of ascertaining the qualifications of voters as to their ability to read and speak the English language, and providing for punishment of persons voting or registering in violation of the provisions of this section."

137 Robert E. Ficken, Washington State: The Inaugural Decade, 1889-1899, (Pullman: Washington State University Press: 2007), 183-185.

138 Silver Republicans advocated free coinage of silver and were against the gold standard for currency, a platform that was attractive to the mining interests in Washington and elsewhere in the West.

139 Martha E. Pike, "Washington," in HWS 4: 972.

140 Marte Jo Sheeran, "The Woman Suffrage Issue in Washington, 1890-1910" (master's thesis, University of Washington, 1977), 28.

141 Barbara Cloud, "Laura Hall Peters: Pursuing the Myth of Equality," Pacific Northwest Quarterly 74, no. 1 (January 1983): 28-36.

142 Peters asked Speaker Charles E. Cline, "a staunch suffragist," to recognize Representative L. E. Rader, who presented the amended bill, which passed the House again by a 54–15 vote.

143 Martha E. Pike, "Washington," in HWS 4: 972.

144 Conventioneers elected Carrie Hill president; Laura Hall Peters vice-president; Martha Pike secretary; and Bessie Savage treasurer.

145 Martha E. Pike, "Washington," in HWS 4: 973.

146 NAWSA formed in 1890 when the NWSA and AWSA, which had split in 1869 over the Fifteenth Amendment, rejoined to mount a two-pronged campaign for women's suffrage.

147 Martha E. Pike, "Washington," in HWS 4: 976.

148 Ibid., 4:973.

149 Sheeran, "Woman Suffrage Issue in Washington," 72, 73.

150 Ibid., 67-68.

151 Ibid., 79, 80.

152 Dr. Cora Smith Eaton King and others, "Washington," in *HWS* 6: 673. Carrie Hill was president of the Equal Suffrage Association from 1898 to 1900; Nena Jolidon Croake of Tacoma was the state president from 1900-1902; Dr. Luema G. Johnson of Tacoma held the office from 1902-1904; and Fannie Leake Cummings of Seattle headed the organization in 1904-1906. Johnson headed labor support for the 1910 amendment. Croake was later elected as one of the first Washington women legislators in 1912.

153 "National American Convention of 1905" in *HWS* 4: 124.

154 For more on this topic, see Ronald Taber, "Sacajawea and the Suffragettes," *Pacific Northwest Quarterly* 58, no. 1 (January 1967): 7-13.

155 Edwards, *Sowing Good Seeds*, 238.

156 According to Susan Strasser in *Never Done: A History of American Housework* (New York: Henry Holt and Company, 1982), 6. "Between about 1890 and 1920, mass production and mass distribution brought new products and services—gas, electricity, running water, prepared foods, ready-made clothes and factory-made furniture and utensils—to a large number of American families."

157 Alice Kessler-Harris, *Out to Work* (Oxford University Press: New York, 1982), 112–116.

158 Nancy Woloch, *Women and the American Experience, Volume Two, From 1860* (New York: McGraw-Hill, 1994), 270.

159 Virginia Scharff, *Taking the Wheel: Women and the Coming of the Motor Age,* (Toronto: Collier Macmillan Canada; Maxwell Mcmillan , International, 1991), 24.

160 Ibid., 87.

161 Robert Cooney, *Winning California for Woman Suffrage* (Santa Rosa, Calif.: National Women's History Project, 2006), 5.

162 Margery W. Davies, *Woman's Place Is At the Typewriter: Office Work and Office workers, 1870–1930* (Philadelphia: Temple University Press, 1982), 52. Also see, Kessler-Harris, *Out to Work*, 147–149.

163 Hoke, Donald, "The Woman and the Typewriter: A Case Study in Technological Innovation and Social Change," Milwaukee Public Museum, www.h-net.org/~business/bhcweb/publications/BEHprint/v008/p0076-p0088.pdf.

164 Davies, *Woman's Place*, 163–175.

165 Kessler-Harris, *Out to Work*, 147–149.

166 Ibid., 139–140.

167 Washington State Supreme Court Chief Justice Gerry Alexander, e-mail message to author, April 4, 2008.

168 Ross-Nazzal, "Always be Good Natured and Cheerful," 121.

169 Larson, "Woman Suffrage Movement in Washington," 56.

170 Eaton King and othrs, "Washington," in *HWS* 6: 674.

171 Ross-Nazzal, "Always be Good Natured and Cheerful," 126.

172 Bagley, *History of Seattle*, vol. 2, 499. A center of activism, the Arcade Building also housed a free dispensary, organized by the Ladies' Hebrew Benevolent Society.

173 Larson, "Woman Suffrage Movement in Washington," 58.

174 C. H. Baily, "How Washington Women Regained the Ballot," *Pacific Monthly* 26 (July 1911): 1-11, 8. See also "Women Play Game of Politics," *Seattle Post-Intelligencer*, October 4, 1908.

175 See Laura Arksey, "In No Uncertain Terms: From the Writings of May Arkwright Hutton," *The Pacific Northwesterner* 52, no. 1 (April 2008): 1-46; Emalee Gruss Gills, "May Arkwright Hutton and the Battle for Women's Suffrage," in *The Pacific Northwest Inlander* (March 6, 2008): 16-21; James W. Montgomery, *Liberated Woman: A Life of May Arkwright Hutton* (Fairfield, Wash.: Ye Galleon Press, 1974); Patricia Voeller Horner, "May Arkwright Hutton: Suffragist and Politician," in *Women in Pacific Northwest History*, ed. Karen J. Blair (Seattle: University of Washington Press, 1988) 25-42; and May Arkwright Hutton Papers, Northwest Museum of Arts & Culture/ Eastern Washington State Historical Society, Spokane, Wash.

176 Russel B. Nye, *Midwestern Progressive Politics* (East Lansing, 1959), 183, quoted in William T. Kerr, "The Progressive of Washington, 1910-12," *Pacific Northwest Quarterly* 55 (January 1964): 16-27, quotation on 16.

177 Mead, *How the Vote Was Won*, 98.

178 *History of Woman Suffrage*, vol. 6, 683.

179 National Women's Hall of Fame, "Women of the Hall—Emma Smith DeVoe," NWHF, http://www.greatwomen.org/women.php?action=viewone&id=46. See also Jennifer Ross-Nazzal, "'Always be Good Natured and Cheerful': Emma Smith DeVoe and the Woman Suffrage Movement" (PhD diss., Washington State University, 2004); Ross-Nazzal "Emma Smith DeVoe: Practicing Pragmatic Politics in the Pacific Northwest," *Pacific Northwest Quarterly* 96, no. 2 (Spring 2005): 76-84; Emma Smith DeVoe Papers, Washington State Library, Olympia.

180 Sheeran, "Woman Suffrage Issue in Washington," 90.

181 Mary Susan Pacey, "The Breakthrough State: The Washington State Suffrage Campaign of 1906-1910," (master's thesis, University of Washington, 1978), 136.

182 "Suffragettes Are Here," *Morning Olympian*, January 14, 1909.

183 Baily, "How Washington Women Regained the Ballot," 9. Among them were Carrie M. Hill, May Arkwright Hutton, Nellie Fick, Edith Delong Jarmuth, Leonia

W. Brown, Maude Parker, Sarah Kendall, Mrs. Ellen S. Leckenby, Bessie Isaacs Savage, sisters Helen, Louise, Gertrude and Lucy Kangley, Adella M. Parker, Mary Quigley, Mary G. O'Meara, Florentine Schage, Margaret O'Meara, Mary A. D. Brennan, Mary Kelley, Irene Walen, Kathryn Smith, Nellie Rininger, and Cora Mellott.

184 "Woman Suffrage Forces Hopeful," *Seattle Post-Intelligencer*, January 15, 1909.

185 "Mrs. Emma Smith DeVoe's Principles for Guidance in Suffrage Campaigns," n.d., National Woman's Party Papers, Library of Congress, Washington, D.C. (microfilm edition, Fondren Library, Rice University); and Ross-Nazzal, "Always be Good Natured and Cheerful," 118. Her full ten principles: 1—Keep the issue single. Be for nothing but suffrage; against nothing but anti-suffrage. 2—Pin your faith to the justice of your cause. It carries conviction. 3—Rely upon facts rather than arguments. 4—Plead affirmative arguments always. Put your opponents on the defensive. 5—Convert the indifferent: there are thousands of them. Let the incorrigible alone; there are only a few. 6—Avoid big meetings; they arouse your enemies. 7—Avoid antagonizing big business, but get the labor vote quietly. 8—Be confident of winning. 9—Try to have every voter in the state asked by some woman to vote for the amendment; this will carry it. 10—Always be good natured and cheerful.

186 Amendment 2 (1896), Wash. Const., art. 6 sec. 1 (Qualification of Voters).

187 Sheeran, "Woman Suffrage Issue in Washington," 89.

188 Eaton to Catt, October 24, 1909, Emma Smith DeVoe Papers, Box 2 Folder 5, Washington State Library, Olympia, Wash.; and Ross-Nazzal, "Always be Good Natured and Cheerful," 147.

189 Governor Samuel Cosgrove was ill and Lieutenant Governor Hay was Acting Governor at this time. Governor Cosgrove died on March 28, 1909.

190 Sheeran, "Woman Suffrage Issue in Washington," 101.

191 Ibid., 107-8.

192 "Correspondence" *Votes for Women* 1, no. 3 (February, 1910): 7.

193 John Putnam, "A 'Test of Chiffon Politics': Gender Politics in Seattle, 1897-1917," in "Woman Suffrage: The View from the Pacific," special issue, *Pacific Historical Review* 69, no. 4 (November 2000): 595-616, esp. 599.

194 "The Spirit of the West," *Votes for Women* 1, no. 1 (October, 1909): 4.

195 Putnam, "Test of Chiffon Politics," 599.

196 Others included Florence Kelley, Laura Clay, Fanny Garrison Villard, and Kate M. Gordon.

197 "National American Convention of 1909," in *HWS* 5: 245.

198 "Twenty-Minutes' Stop Full of Festivities," *Seattle Times*, June 29, 1909.

199 Clippings, scrapbook 3, box 3, May Arkwright Hutton Papers, Eastern Washington Historical Society, Spokane, Wash.; and Ross-Nazzal, "Always be Good Natured and Cheerful," 152.

200 Pacey, "Breakthrough State," 151-52. Among the women were Edith Jarmuth, Cora Mellott, Leonia Brown, and LaReine Baker.

201 Eaton to Hutton, June 17, 1909, box 2, folder 5, DeVoe Papers.

202 Other officers of the EFS were: Nellie Fick and Mrs. D. L. Carmichael, assistants; Flora S. Bash, corresponding secretary; Mrs. W. T. Perkins, recording secretary; Nellie Rininger, treasurer; and Phebe A. Ryan, financial secretary. Others who worked without pay were Martha Gruening of New York and Jeannette Rankin of Montana.

203 Putnam, "Test of Chiffon Politics," 598.

204 "Suffragettes Are Stirring Spokane," *Walla Walla Statesman*, July 15, 1909.

205 Finland enacted women's suffrage in 1906; Norway in 1907.

206 Margaret Riddle and Louise Lindgren, "Snohomish County Women and the 1910 Suffrage Campaign," "Women's Stories—Women's Lives, The Snohomish County Women's Legacy Project, Everett Public Library, http://www.snocoheritage.org/wlp_46_Suffrage.html.

207 Karen J. Blair, "The Limits of Sisterhood: the Woman's Building in Seattle, 1908-1921," in *Women in Pacific Northwest History: An Anthology*, ed. Karen Blair (Seattle: University of Washington Press, 1988), 170.

208 Alice Blackwell, "National American Convention of 1909," in *HWS* 5: 264-5.

209 Ibid.

210 "Suffragists Hold Love Feast," *Edmonds Review*, July 17, 1909. See also http://www.historylink.org/ files on women's suffrage at the AYPE.

211 Sheeran, "Woman Suffrage Issue in Washington," 135.

212 Mead, *How the Vote Was Won*, 112, 114; *Spokane Inland Herald*, September 3, 1910; *Spokane Chronicle*, November 5, 1910.

213 "National American Convention of 1909," in *HWS* 5: 260. "Mrs. (Florence) Kelley spoke in the First Christian Church, Mrs. Eva Emery Dye in the Second Avenue Congregational Church and the Rev. Mary G. Andrews preached for the Universalists on The Freedom of Truth. At the First Methodist Protestant Church, Miss Laura Clay talked on Christian Citizenship in the morning and Dr. Shaw preached in the evening. Mrs. Charlotte Perkins Gilman spoke at the Boylston Avenue Unitarian Church in the morning and Mrs. Gilman and Mrs.

Pauline Steinem at a patriotic service in Plymouth Church in the evening. Mr. Blackwell and Mrs. Steinem spoke in the Jewish synagogue."

214 "Suffrage at African-Methodist Conference," *Votes for Women* 1, no. 9–10 (Aug.–Sept., 1910): 5.

215 Martha Offerdahl and Ida M. Abelset composed the Scandinavian booklet.

216 Eaton King and others, "Washington" in *HWS* 6: 679.

217 Dale Soden, *The Reverend Mark Matthews: An Activist in the Progressive Era* (Seattle: University of Washington Press, 2001), 100.

218 "Bishop Attacks New Woman," *Ellensburg Record*, July 14, 1909.

219 "Will be Mecca of the Suffragists," *Spokane Chronicle*, July 14, 1909.

220 Mead, *How the Vote Was Won*, 113–14.

221 The speakers included Jessie Atkinson, Ethel Stalford, and Rose Bassett Moore.

222 Eaton King and others, "Washington," in *HWS* 6: 678.

223 Ross-Nazzal, "Always be Good Natured and Cheerful," 132.

224 Charles Simon Barett, *The Mission History and Times of the Farmer's Union* (Nashville: Marshall & Bruce Co., 1909), 245–46.

225 "Progress of the Campaign Through the State," *Votes for Women* 1, no. 10 (October, 1910): 14.

226 "Too Aggressive, Hurt Cause of the Women," DeVoe Scrapbook, 8, Box 9, DeVoe Papers, n.p., n.d.; and Ross-Nazzal, "Always be Good Natured and Cheerful," 143.

227 Frances M. Bjorkman, "Women's Political Methods," *Collier's*, August 20, 1910, 23–24; and Ross-Nazzal, "Always be Good Natured and Cheerful," 143.

228 Dr. Cora Smith Eaton King, "How Washington Women Won the Vote," *The Forecast*, 351, n.d., in Cora Smith Eaton King Scrapbook, DeVoe Papers.

229 Ibid., 352.

230 *Votes for Women* 1, no. 1 (October, 1909): 4.

231 Poster brigades were in Seattle, Tacoma, Bellingham, Olympia, Spokane, Walla Walla, Ellensburg, White Salmon, Columbus, Sheridan, Wilson Creek, White Bluffs, Ritzville, Thorp, Roslyn, Port Orchard, Riverside, Prosser, Starbuck, Pomeroy, Asotin, Clarkston, Pasco, Waitsburg, Prescott, Wallula, Burbank, Popez, Richardson, Dayton, Little Falls, Manette, Aberdeen, Chehalis, Sunnyside, Langley, Snohomish, Grandview, Goldendale, Luzon, Port Gamble, Cunningham, Olalla, Home, Rosedale, Lakebay, and Cromwell.

232 Mead, *How the Vote Was Won*, 112.

233 Elizabeth Baker in Kitsap; Ida Agnes Baker in Whatcom; Mariella Welch in Cowlitz; Linda Jennings in Skagit; Anna E. Goodwin in King; and Louise Cummings in Wallula.

234 "Woman Suffrage Bound to Come," *Votes for Women* 1, no. 7 (June 1910): 4.

235 Eaton King and others, "Washington," in *HWS* 6: 678.

236 List of newspapers in support of suffrage: *Grays Harbor Post* (Aberdeen); *Aberdeen Herald*; *Anacortes American*; *Arlington Times*; *Auburn Republican*; *Bellingham Reveille*; *Bremerton Navy Yard American*; *Cheney Free Press*; *Colfax Commoner*; *Ellensburg Capital*; *Elma Chronicle*; *Everett Herald*; *Friday Harbor San Juan Islander*; *Goldendale Sentinel*; *Grays Harbor Washingtonian* (Hoquiam); *Kelso Kelsonian*; *Kennewick Reporter*; *Mount Vernon Argus*; *Okanogan Independent*; *Olympia Morning Olympian*; *Olympia Washington Standard*; *Pasco Progress*; *Pasco Express*; *Port Angeles Tribune Times*; *Port Angeles Olympic Leader*; *Puyallup Valley Tribune*; *Seattle Star*; *Times*; *Seattle Post-Intelligencer*, *Seattle Week End*; *Seattle Republican*; *Skagit County Courier* (Sedro Woolley); *South Bend Journal*; *Spokane Spokesman Review*; *Spokane Western Farmer*, *Spokane Chronicle*; *The Sun* (Sunnyside); *Tacoma News-Ledger*, *Tacoma Tribune*; *Tacoma New Herald*; *Vancouver Independent Chronicle*; *Vashon Island News*; *Walla Walla Bulletin*; *The Enterprise* (White Salmon). "Notes and Correspondence on History," box 5, folder 5, DeVoe Papers,

237 "Memorial Services in Honor of Henry B. Blackwell," *Votes for Women* 1, no. 1 (October, 1909) 2.

238 "The Poll List Canvass," *Votes for Women* 1, no. 7 (June, 1910): 7. Compiled from *Votes for Women*. "A complete list of the workers who are taking part in this tremendous piece of work is not at hand, but a partial list follows: Vashon Island, Chautauqua—Mrs. Frances Scott Cliff; Burton—Mrs. S. L. W. Clark; Pierce—Mrs. Annie Beadle; Cowlitz—Mariella Welch, Mrs. Carrie Buchanan Roberts; Kitsap—Mrs. Elizabeth Baker; Klickitat—Mrs. Jennie Jewett; Clarke—Mrs. Margaret Heyes Hall; Grant—Mrs. May Stanley; Whatcom—Mrs. Dora W. Cryderman; Thurston—Miss Bernice Sapp; Lewis—Mrs. Eunolia B. Mullen, Mrs. Anna Lafferty; Mason—Mrs. Annie C. Curie, Mrs. Marie B. Kneeland, Mrs. Mary C. Willey, Mrs. Irene S. Reed; Chehalis—Mrs. J. M. Walker; Walla Walla—Mrs. Lucie F. Isaacs."

239 Mead, *How the Vote Was Won*, 155.

240 While in Congress, Rankin voted against declaration of war for World War I and was the only dissenting vote in Congress for declaration of World War II.

241 "The Franchise Departments," *Votes for Women* 1, no. 10 (October, 1910): 25. Active WCTU officers included eastern Washington superintendent Mary Yeager and western Washington superintendent Mrs. S. L. W. Clark; Margaret B. Platt, WCTU state president; and Margaret C. Munns, WCTU state secretary.

242 Eaton King and others, "Washington," in *HWS* 6: 680.

243 Mrs. George A. (Kathryn) Smith, "Jubilee Night at the National Convention," *New Citizen* 2, no. 18 (January 1912): 3.

244 Eaton King and others, "Washington," in *HWS* 6: 680.

245 Smith, "Jubilee Night at the National Convention," *New Citizen* 2, no. 18 (January 1912): 3.

246 Mead, *How the Vote Was Won*, 112, 115.

247 Mead, *How the Vote Was Won*, 115.

248 The group included Asahel Curtis, L. A. Nelson, Lulie Nettleton, W. M. Price, Grant W. Humes, F. O. Morrill, P. M. McGregor, E. W. Harnden, Prof. E. S. Meany, Nita J. Feree, Wayne Sensenig, Dr. Cora Smith Eaton King, Lydia E. Lovering, Winona Bailey, G. D. Emerson, Dr. E. F. Stevens, John A. Best Jr., Roy Hurd, Mary J. Price, Henry Howard, H. C. Belt, Mrs. H. C. Belt, John Fahnstock, C. M. Farrer, Annie Farrer, Lulie Smith, Olaf Hansen, Charles Albertson, Dr. F. J. Van Horn, May I. Dwyer, Anna Howard, S. L. Moyer, Elizabeth David, H. Hutchinson, R. Merrill, Alida J. Bigelow, Blake D. Mills, Cora Garvin, Robert Van Horn, Dr. L. W. Clark, Stella Scholes, J. M. Jensen, Bertha Reed, H. V. Abel, Gladys M. Tuttle, Murray McLean, Freda Sanford, Grace Howard, Rena Raymond, Anna Stauber, H. May Baptie, A. W. Archer, Mollie Leckenby, Robert Carr, Lawrence Carr, J. Fred Black, H. Otto Knispel, Major E. S. Ingraham, Kenneth Ingraham, Richard Buck, W. J. Colkett, Harvey Moore. See Paula Becker, "Suffragists Join The Mountaineers' Club 1909 Outing to Mount Rainier and Plant an A-Y-P Exposition Flag and a 'Votes For Women' Banner at the Summit of Columbia Crest on July 30, 1909," HistoryLink, http://www.historylink.org/index.cfm?DisplayPage=output.cfm&File_Id=8578; and Asahel Curtis, "Mountaineers' Outing to Mount Rainier," *The Mountaineer* 2 (November 1909): 4-15.

249 L. A. Nelson, "Ascent of Mt. Olumpus," The Mountaineers, http://www.mountaineers.org/seattle/climbing/Reference/1907OlympusFA.html.

250 "Excelsior—Carrying Suffrage's Banner Up Mt. Rainier," *Seattle Sunday Times*, August 23, 1908, Magazine Section.

251 "Mrs. Baker's Pike's Peak Feat," *Spokane Spokesman-Review*, November 14, 1909; and "Airs Suffrage on Peak and in Mine," *Spokane Chronicle*, November 20, 1909.

252 "Cool Things: American Woman and Her Political Peers," Kansas State Historical Society, http://www.kshs.org/cool/coolamwm.htm.

253 "Decries Militant Suffrage Crusade," *Spokesman Review* [?], November 1, 1909.

254 Sheeran, "Woman Suffrage Issue in Washington," 130.

255 Eaton King and others, "Washington," in *HWS* 6: 681.

256 Eaton King, "'The Anti's' and Dr. Matthews." Notes and Correspondence on History, 1919-20, DeVoe Papers.

257 "Progress of the Campaign Over the State," *Votes for Women* 1, no. 6 (May, 1910): 9.

258 Sheeran, "Woman Suffrage Issue in Washington," 143.

259 Larson, "Woman Suffrage Movement in Washington," 61.

260 Baily, "How Washington Women Regained the Ballot," 10.

261 HWS 6:682. Eastern contributors included Henry B. Blackwell and Alice Stone Blackwell, Mass., $250; Mr. and Mrs. J. H. Lesser, California, $100; Mrs. H. E. Flansburg, New York, $100; Miss Janet Richards, Washington, D.C., $100; the Rev. Olympia Brown, Wisconsin, $25. Contributions to the Equal Franchise Society included $200 from Fanny Garrison Villard, $250 from Mrs. Susan Look Avery, of Kentucky; $300 from Mrs. Elizabeth Smith Miller and Miss Anne Fitzhugh Miller of New York, as well as several other eastern contributors—about $3,000 in all.

262 "Don't Forget to Vote for the Amendments at the Top of the Ballot," *Votes for Women* 1, no. 10 (October, 1910): 23.

263 Eaton King and others, "Washington," in *HWS* 6: 675.

264 "The Great Victory in Washington," *Votes for Women* 1, no. 11 (December, 1910): 1.

265 Sheeran, "Woman Suffrage Issue in Washington," 144.

266 Only 59.3 percent of those casting ballots in the general election voted on the suffrage issue. The reason for this anomaly is unknown, but the ballot wording may have confused some voters.

267 Sheeran, "Woman Suffrage Issue in Washington," 149-50.

268 "Women Are to Give Special Thanks," November 13, 1910, newspaper clipping, n.p., DeVoe Scrapbooks, DeVoe Papers.

269 "Women of State Get Ballot By Gift of Men," *Seattle Post-Intelligencer*, November 10, 1910, 11.

270 "Women Are to Give Special Thanks," November 13, 1910, newspaper clipping, n.p., DeVoe Scrapbooks, DeVoe Papers.

271 Putnam, "Test of Chiffon Politics," 605.

272 Mead, *How the Vote Was Won*, 99.

273 David Hastings, Washington State Archives, e-mail message to author, December 3, 2008. In 1908 the votes for all gubernatorial candidates was 176,171 and in 1912

the total was 318,359, which indicates a major increase; David Leip, "United States Presidential Election Results," http://uselectionatlas.org/RESULTS/index.html. The number of votes cast in Washington for U.S. president in 1908 was 183,879, while in 1912 the total was 322,799; Atlas of U.S. Presidential Elections,

274 Kerr, "The Progressives of Washington," 16.

275 Margaret V. Sherlock, "The Recall of Mayor Gill," *Pacific Monthly* 26, no. 2 (August 1911), 117-30.

276 Putnam, "Test of Chiffon Politics," 607.

277 Nancy F. Cott, "Across the Great Divide," in *One Women, One Vote*, ed. Marjorie Sprull Wheeler (Troutdale, Ore.: New Sage Press, 1995), 360.

278 Mrs. S. L. Clark, Mrs. John Trumbull, Mrs. R. F. Weeks, and Rosetta Silbaugh were Federation lobbyists who worked with Leslie Wallace of the WCTU.

279 Marianne Lippincott, "Women's Legislative Council of Washington, November, 1917 to May 1938," unpublished manuscript, 1980, Central Washington University, Ellensburg, Wash.

280 Putnam, "Test of Chiffon Politics," 608. However, it became an official paper of the American Woman's League which was for "Caucasian women only."

281 Ibid., 612.

282 See Appendix A for a summary of reform legislation during these years.

283 Kathryn J. Oberdeck, "'Not Pink Teas': The Seattle Working-Class Women's Movement, 1905-1918," *Labor History*, 32 (1991): 193-230, esp. 197. This article is an important summary of the women's labor movement in Seattle during this period. See also Putnam, "Test of Chiffon Politics," 609-11.

284 Putnam, "Test of Chiffon Politics," 615. According to Putnam, "the cross-class alliance that clubwomen forged with organized labor, initially founded upon a shared concern about the plight of working women, slowly collapsed under the weight of class conflict."

285 Information for this section comes from Michael Reese, "To Help Her Live the Right Kind of Life—Mothers' Pensions in King County, 1913-1937," in *More Voices, New Stories: King County, Washington's First 150 Years*. Project of the Pacific Northwest Historians Guild, 189-214, ed. Mary C. Wright (Seattle: King County Landmarks & Heritage Commission, 2002).

286 Michael Reese, e-mail message to author, August 28, 2008.

287 Margaret Riddle, "Washington State Senate Approves a Women's Eight-Hour Workday on March 2, 1911," HistoryLink, http://www.historylink.org/index.cfm?DisplayPage=output.cfm&file_id=8315.

288 Kessler-Harris, *Out to Work*, 188-89.

289 Riddle, "Washington State Senate Approves," http://www.historylink.org/index.cfm?DisplayPage=output.cfm&file_id=8315.

290 "Alice Lord," author unknown, Alice Lord Manuscript Collection, MS 198, Washington State Historical Society, Tacoma.

291 Norman H. Clark, *The Dry Years: Prohibition and Social Change in Washington*, (Seattle: University of Washington Press, 1988): 90-91.

292 Information adapted from Clark, *Dry Years*.

293 Clark, *Dry Years*, 113.

294 Ross-Nazzal, "Always be Good Natured and Cheerful," 169. The organization may also have been part of the disaffection of western states with NAWSA.

295 Ibid., 168.

296 Ibid., 169-70. I wish to acknowledge Ross-Nazzal's work on establishing the importance of the National Council of Women Voters in the passage of the federal amendment.

297 *Tacoma News Tribune*, January 13, 1911, quoted in Ross-Nazzal, "Always be Good Natured and Cheerful," 171.

298 Ross-Nazzal, "Always be Good Natured and Cheerful," 176.

299 Whether King marched in the March 3 parade is unknown—her obituary and a family reminiscence indicate that she might have participated. See Jean Gardiner Smith to George W. Starcher, January 9, 1963, in the files from the President of the University of North Dakota, provided to the author by the University of North Dakota.

300 "Suffrage Autoists Besiege Senators; Motor Parade From Hyattsville, Md., Precedes Presentation of Petitions at Capitol. Special to the *New York Times*," *New York Times*, August 1, 1913, 7.

301 DeVoe to King, September 2, 1914, NWP Papers; and Ross-Nazzal, "Always be Good Natured and Cheerful," 198.

302 Inez Haynes Irwin, *The Story of Alice Paul and the National Woman's Party* (1921; repr., Fairfax, Va.: Denlingers Publishers, Inc., 1977), 156-57.

303 "Origin of Suffrage Colors: Early Campaigns," *Votes for Women* 1, no. 10 (October, 1910): 29.

304 National Women's History Museum, "An Introduction to the Woman's Suffrage Movement," National Women's History Museum, http://www.nmwh.org/exhibits/tour_1.html.

305 Linda G. Ford, "Alice Paul and the Triumph of Militancy," in *One Woman, One Vote*, ed. Marjorie Spruill Wheeler (Troutdale, Ore.: New Sage Press, 1995).

306 Library of Congress, American Memory, "Women of Protest: Photographs from the Records of the National Woman's Party," http://memory.loc.gov/ammem/collections/suffrage/nwp/index.html.

307 Robert Booth Fowler, "Carrie Chapman Catt, Strategist," in *One Woman, One Vote*, ed. Marjorie Spruill Wheeler (Troutdale, Ore.: New Sage Press, 1995); and Woloch, *Women and the American Experience*, 2:353.

308 "Suffrage Amendment Ratified Unanimously," *Washington Standard*, March 23, 1920, 1.

309 Eaton King and others, "Washington," in *HWS* 6: 685-86.

310 Nineteenth Amendment, http://www.archives.gov/ exhibits/featured_documents/amendment_19/ print_friendly.html?page=index_content. html&title=The_19th_Amendment

311 Ross-Nazzal, "Always be Good Natured and Cheerful," 211.

312 Jill Severn, *The State We're In: Washington, Your guide to state, tribal and local government*, (Seattle: The League of Women Voters Education Fund, 2004), 36.

313 Washington State Constitution, art. 6, Washington State Legislature, http://www.leg.wa.gov/ LawsAndAgencyRules/constitution.htm.

314 League of Women Voters, "About the League," http:// www.lwv.org/AM/Template.cfm?Section=About_Us (accessed November 8, 2008).

315 *National League for Woman's Service Washington State Report for 1917-1919*, n.p., n.d.

316 This was particularly true in bond sales, see Ellis Report below.

317 WASHINGTON STATE LEGISLATURE, STATE COUNCIL OF DEFENSE, "A Report of the Women's Liberty Loan Committee of the State of Washington for the Second, Third, and Fourth Liberty Loans," in *Report of the State Council of Defense Covering Its Activities During the War, June 16, 1917, to January 9, 1919*, by Jennie Wilhite Ellis (Olympia, 1919), 122; and Ellis, "Report of the Women's Committee of the State of Washington for the Victory Liberty Loan Campaign, April 7 to May 10, 1919," MS 72, box 1, folder 3, Washington State Historical Society, Tacoma.

318 Ruth Karr McKee, "Woman's Work in Connection With War Activities" in *Report of the State Council of Defense Covering Its Activities During the War, June 16, 1917, to January 9, 1919*

319 *National League for Woman's Service Washington State Report for 1917–1919.*

320 John Hartl, "Witness to Revolution: Anna Louise Strong," Communism in Washington State History and Memory Project, Pacific Northwest Labor History Project, http://depts.washington.edu/labhist/ cpproject/Witness.htm.

321 Ellen Carol Dubois, *Woman Suffrage and Women's Rights* (New York: New York University Press, 1998), 217.

322 Sandra Haarsager, *Bertha Knight Landes of Seattle: Big City Mayor* (Norman: University of Oklahoma Press, 1994).

323 Doris Pieroth, "Bertha Knight Landes: The Woman Who Was Mayor," in *Women in Pacific Northwest History*, ed. Karen J. Blair, rev. ed. ([1988] Seattle: University of Washington Press, 2001), 154.

324 Alex McBride, "*West Coast Hotel v. Parrish* (1937)" U.S. Supreme Court Landmark Cases, Educational Broadcasting Corporation, http://www.pbs.org/wnet/ supremecourt/capitalism/landmark_westcoast.html.

325 WW II Voices in the Classroom, "The Voices of World War II," Bristol Productions, Ltd., http://www. wwiihistoryclass.com/documentaries/women.html.

326 Leila J. Rupp and Verta Taylor, *Survival in the Doldrums: The American Women's Rights Movement, 1945 to the 1960s*, (New York: Oxford University Press, 1987), 13.

327 Glenda Riley, *Inventing the American Woman: An Inclusive History*, vol. 2, *Since 1877* (Wheeling, Ill.: Harlan Davidson, 2001), 476.

328 Leila J. Rupp and Verta Taylor, *Survival in the Doldrums*, 7.

329 Ibid., 45-84. See page 46 for a list of women's groups.

330 Janine A. Parry, "Putting Feminism to a Vote," *Pacific Northwest Quarterly* 91, no. 4 (Fall 2000): 171-82, esp. 172.

331 See Appendix B for a summary chronology of changes of women's rights during the period.

332 Susan Paynter, "The Fight for Equal Rights: A Fifty-Year Struggle for Change," *Seattle Post-Intelligencer*, July 30, 1972, to August 11, 1972.

333 "Equal Rights Amendments: State Provisions," CRS Report for Congress, Order Code RS20217, updated August 23, 2004.

334 Alice Paul Institute, "The Equal Rights Amendment, a Brief Introduction," equalrightsamendment.org, http:// www.equalrightsamendment.org/overview.htm.

335 Jean Withers, Lynn Morrison, Ruth Jones, and Fredericka Foster, *The Women of Ellensburg, Report of the Washington State International Women's Year Conference*, n.p., 1977. See also Washington Women's History Consortium, "WHC IWY Oral History Project," http://www. washingtonwomenshistory.org/themes/womensrights/ oHistProj.aspx.

336 Parry, "Putting Feminism to a Vote," 177

337 Hannelore Suderman, "History Was Made . . . The Fight for Equity for Women's Athletics in Washington," *Washington State Magazine* (Winter 2007-08), http:// washington-state-magazine.wsu.edu/stories/2007/ November/history.html.

338 Cassandra Tate, "Abortion Reform in Washington State," February 26, 2003, HistoryLink.org, http:// www.historylink.org/essays/output.cfm?file_id=5313; Cassandra Tate, "Dr. Samual Goldenberg Recalls the Campaign to Liberalize Washington's Abortion Laws," January 1, 1900 [*sic*], HistoryLink.org, http:// www.historylink.org/essays/output.cfm?file_id=2656; Cassandra Tate, "Lee Minto, Director of Planned

Parenthood from 1967 to 1993, Recalls the History of Abortion Reform," January 1, 1900 [*sic*], HistoryLink.org, http://www.historylink.org/essays/output.cfm?file_id=2643, and Cassandra Tate, "Marilyn Ward Recalls the Campaign to Reform Washington's Abortion Law," January 1, 1900 [*sic*], HistoryLink.org, http://www.historylink.org/essays/output.cfm?file_id=2675.

339 Washington Federation of State Employees, "A History of Comparable Worth as Initiated by the Washington Federation of State Employees, AFSCME, Council 28, http://www.geocities.com/judgetanner/cw.htm (accessed April 3, 2009; the original WFSE/AFSCME site for this document has been discontinued).

340 The Catherine May Bedell Papers are available through the Women's History Consortium Web site at www.WashingtonWomensHistory.org.

341 See Appendix C for a summary of women's legislative history and a list of women elected statewide in Washington.

342 Adella Parker, abstractor, "Laws of Washington of Interest to Women Passed Since the Adoption of Suffrage, November, 1910," box 5, folder 4, DeVoe Papers.

343 Compiled from Washington State Women's Council information and other sources.

344 Center for American Women and Politics, Eagleton Institute of Politics, Rutgers, The State University of New Jersey, New Brunswick.

345 Ibid.

Sources

*T*he following sources are included to furnish the reader and researcher with an extensive list of reference materials. Some of these sources, notably the Emma Smith DeVoe and May Arkwright Hutton papers and scrapbooks, are part of the Washington Women's History Consortium's online resources at WashingtonWomensHistory.org. Many of these references place the Washington suffrage campaigns in a broader historical context while others provide diverse perspectives on the campaign at various points in time. Using these materials, readers can go beyond this publication to investigate the larger sphere of women's history.

COLLECTIONS:

Alice Lord Manuscript Collection. Washington State Historical Society, Tacoma.

Emma Smith DeVoe Papers. Washington State Library, Everett.

Jenner Family Collection. Private collection.

May Arkwright Hutton Papers. Eastern Washington State Historical Society, Cheney.

Susan B. Anthony Papers. Library of Congress, Washington, D.C. (microfilm edition available).

Women's History Collection. Washington State Historical Society, Tacoma.

LEGAL CASES:

Bradwell v. Illinois, 18 U.S. 130 (1873).

Slaughterhouse Cases, 83 U.S. 36 (1873).

Minor v. Happersett, 88 U.S. 162 (1875).

Hays v. Territory of Washington, 2 Wash. Terr. 286, 5P. 927 (1884).

Rosencrantz v. Territory of Washington, 2 Wash. Terr. 267 (1884).

George Schilling v. Territory of Washington, 2 Wash. Terr. 283 (1884).

Walker v. Territory of Washington, 2 Wash. Terr. 186 5P. 313 (1884).

Harland v. Territory of Washington, 3 Wash. Terr. 131 (1887).

Bloomer v. Todd, 3 Wash. Terr. 599 (1888).

Thornton v. Territory of Washington, 3 Wash. Terr. 48. (1888)

STATUTES:

Statute Law Committee. *Revised Code of Washington 26.16.030.* Olympia, 2008.

Washington Territorial Legislature. *Acts of the Legislative Assembly.* Olympia: Furste, 1858.

Washington Territorial Legislature. *Laws of Washington Territory.* Olympia: T. F. McElroy, 1867.

Washington Territorial Legislature. *Laws of Washington Territory.* Olympia: Bagley, 1877.

Washington Territorial Legislature. *Laws of Washington Territory.* Olympia: Cavanaugh, 1886.

Washington Territorial Legislature. *Laws of Washington Territory.* Olympia: Cavanaugh, 1888.

Washington Territorial Legislature. *Statutes of Washington Territory.* Olympia: Goudy, 1855.

Washington Territorial Legislature. *Statutes of Washington Territory.* Olympia: Barnes, 1863.

Washington Territorial Legislature. *Statutes of Washington Territory.* Olympia: McElroy, 1866.

Washington Territorial Legislature. *Statutes of Washington Territory.* Olympia: Prosch-McElroy, 1871.

Washington State Legislature. *Washington State Session Laws.* Olympia: White 1889–1890.

Washington State Legislature. *Washington State Session Laws.* Olympia: White, 1895.

Washington Territorial Legislature. Council, 1st sess. *Journal of the Council, Territory of Washington.* Olympia, 1854.

Washington Territorial Legislature. House of Representatives, 1st sess. *Journal of the House, Territory of Washington.* Olympia, 1854.

ELECTRONIC SOURCES:

Andrews, Mildred. "Women Win School Suffrage on March 27, 1890." HistoryLink. http://www.historylink.org/index.cfm?DisplayPage=output.cfm&file_id=469.

Becker, Paula. "Suffragists Join The Mountaineers' Club 1909 Outing to Mount Rainier and Plant an A-Y-P Exposition Flag and a 'Votes For Women' Banner at the Summit of Columbia Crest on July 30, 1909." HistoryLink. http://www.historylink.org/index.cfm?DisplayPage=output.cfm&file_Id=8578.

Crowley, Walt. "Anti-Chinese Activism—Seattle." HistoryLink. http://www.historylink.org/essays/output.cfm?file_id=1057.

Early Office Museum. "Gender and the Office." *Early Office Museum.* http://www.earlyofficemuseum.com/office_gender.htm.

Hartl, John. "Witness to the Revolution: The Story of Anna Louis Strong." Communism in Washington State History and Memory Project. Harry Bridges Center for Labor Studies, University of Washington. http://depts.washington.edu/labhist/cpproject/Witness.htm.

McBride, Alex. "*West Coast Hotel v. Parrish* (1937)." Educational Broadcasting Corporation. http://www.pbs.org/wnet/supremecourt/capitalism/landmark_westcoast.html.

Riddle, Margaret and Louis Lindgren. "Snohomish Women and the 1910 Suffrage Campaign." Women's Stories, Women's Lives: The Snohomish County Women's Legacy Project. Everett Public Library. http://www.snocoheritage.org/wlp_46_Suffrage.html.

———. "Washington State Senate Approves a Women's Eight-hour Workday on March 2, 1911."

HistoryLink. http://www.historylink.org/index.cfm?DisplayPage=output.cfm&file_id=8315.

Library of Congress American Memory. "Women of Protest, Photographs from the Records of the National Woman's Party." Library of Congress. http://memory.loc.gov/ammem/collections/suffrage/nwp/index.html.

Linder, Doug. "The Trial of Susan B. Anthony for Illegal Voting." University of Missouri–Kansas City School of Law. http://www.law.umkc.edu/faculty/projects/ftrials/anthony/sbaaccount.html

Long, Priscilla. "Tacoma Expels the Entire Chinese Community on November 3, 1885." HistoryLink. http://www.historylink.org/essays/output.cfm?file_id=5063.

Malowney, Georgeann. "Justice William Henry White." redmondwashington.org. http://www.redmondwashington.org/biography/white/white-william-henry.htm.

National Women's Rights Historic Park. "Declaration of Sentiments." National Park Service. http://www.nps.gov/wori/historyculture/declaration-of-sentiments.htm.

———. "Report of the Women's Rights Convention." National Park Service. http://www.nps.gov/wori/historyculture/report-of-the-womans-rights-convention.htm

Women's Legal History Biography Project. "Robinson, Lelia (Sawtelle)." Robert Crown Law Library, Stanford Law School. http://womenslegalhistory.stanford.edu/profiles/RobinsonLelia.html.

Tate, Casandra. "Abortion Reform in Washington State." HistoryLink. http://www.historylink.org/essays/output.cfm?file_id=5313.

———. "Dr. Samual Goldenberg recalls the campaign to Liberalize Washington's Abortion Laws." HistoryLink. http://www.historylink.org/essays/output.cfm?file_id=2656.

———. "Lee Minto, Director of Planned Parenthood from 1967 to 1993, Recalls the History of Abortion Reform." HistoryLink. http://www.historylink.org/essays/output.cfm?file_id=2643.

———. "Marilyn Ward Recalls the Campaign to Reform Washington's Abortion Law." HistoryLink. http://www.historylink.org/essays/output.cfm?file_id=2675.

Washington Federation of State Employees. "A History of Comparable Worth as Initiated by the Washington Federation of State Employees, AFSCME, Council 28." http://www.geocities.com/judgetanner/cw.htm.

Washington Women's History Consortium. http://www.washingtonwomenshistory.org/default.aspx.

Whatcom Museum of History and Art Local History Biographies. "The Eldridge Family: Edward Eldridge (1829–1892)." Whatcom Museum of History and Art. http://www.whatcommuseum.org/pages/history/eldridge.htm.

Wiggins, Charles K. "John P. Hoyt & Women Suffrage." Wiggins & Masters. http://www.c-wiggins.com/constitution/hoyt.html.

———. "Charles S. Voorhees and the Omnibus Admissions Act." Wiggins & Masters. http://www.appeal-law.com/constitution/voorhees.html.

ARTICLES AND BOOKS:

Allen, Mrs. John B. "A Plea for the Right of Suffrage to be Restored to the Women of the State of Washington," pamphlet, n.d. Emma Smith DeVoe Collection. Washington State Library, Olympia.

Andrews, Thomas R., Karen Boxx, Ann Murphy, and Gary C. Randall, eds. *Washington Community Property Deskbook*, 3rd ed. Olympia: Washington State Bar Association, 2003.

Arksey, Laura. "In No Uncertain Terms: From the Writings of May Arkwright Hutton." *The Pacific Northwesterner* 52, no. 1 (April 2008): 1–46.

Ault, Nelson A. "The Earnest Ladies: The Walla Walla Woman's Club and the Equal Suffrage League of 1886–1889." *Pacific Northwest Quarterly* 42 (1951): 123–37.

Bagley, Clarence. *History of Seattle*, 3 vols. Seattle: S. J. Clark Publishing Co., 1916.

Bailey, C. H. "How Washington Women Regained the Ballot." *Pacific Monthly* 26 (July 1911): 1–11.

Barett, Charles Simon. *The Mission History and Times of the Farmer's Union*. Nashville, Tenn.: Marshall & Bruce Co., 1909.

Beeton, Beverly. "How the West Was Won for Woman Suffrage." In *One Woman, One Vote: Rediscovering the Women's Suffrage Movement*, edited by Marjorie Spruill Wheeler, 99–116. Troutdale, Ore.: NewSage Press, 1995.

Bjorkman, Frances M. "Women's Political Methods." *Collier's*, 20 August, 1910.

Blair, Karen. "The Limits of Sisterhood: The Woman's Building in Seattle, 1908–1921." In *Women in Pacific Northwest History: An Anthology*, edited by Karen Blair, 65–82. Seattle: University of Washington Press, 1988.

———. *The Clubwoman as Feminist: True Womanhood Redefined, 1868–1914*. New York: Holmes & Meier Publishers, 1988.

Caplan, Aaron. "The History of Women's Jury Service in Washington." *Washington State Bar News* (March 2005): 12–21.

Chused, Richard H. "The Oregon Donation Act of 1850 and Nineteenth-Century Federal Married Women's Property Law." *Law and History Review* 2 (Spring 1984): 44–78.

Clark, Norman. *The Dry Years: Prohibition and Social Change in Washington*. Seattle: University of Washington Press, 1965.

Cloud, Barbara. "Laura Hall Peters: Pursuing the Myth of Equality." *Pacific Northwest Quarterly* 74, no. 1 (January 1983): 28–36.

Colby, Clara Bewick. *The Woman's Tribune*, April 1–June 29, 1889.

Cooney, Robert. *Winning California for Woman Suffrage*. Santa Rosa: National Women's History Project, 2006.

Curtis, Asahel. "Mountaineers' Outing to Mount Rainier." *The Mountaineer* 2 (November 1909): 4–15.

Drury, Clifford. "The Columbia Maternal Association." *Oregon Historical Quarterly* 39 (June 1938): 99–122.

Dubois, Ellen Carol. *Woman Suffrage and Women's Rights*. New York: New York University Press, 1998.

———. "Taking the Law into Our Own Hands." In *One Woman, One Vote*, edited by Marjorie Spruill Wheeler, 81–98. Troutdale, Ore.: NewSage Press, 1996.

Duniway, Abigail Scott. *Path Breaking*. Portland: James, Kerns & Abbott Co., 1914.

Eaton, Cora Smith. "How Washington Women Won the Vote." *The Forecast*. N.p., n.d. Cora Smith Eaton King Scrapbook, ESD Collection. Washington State Library, Everett.

Edwards, G. Thomas. *Sowing Good Seeds: The Northwest Suffrage Campaigns of Susan B. Anthony*. Portland: Oregon Historical Society Press, 1990.

Ellis, Jennie Wilhite. "A Report of the Women's Liberty Loan Committee of the State of Washington for the Second, Third, and Fourth Liberty Loans." In *Report of the State Council of Defense Covering Its Activities during the War, June 16, 1917 to January 9, 1919*. Olympia: Washington State Legislature, 1919.

———. "Report of the Women's Committee of the State of Washington for the Victory Liberty Loan Campaign, April 7, to May 10th, 1919." In MS 72, Box 1 Folder 3. Washington State Historical Society, Tacoma.

Epperson, Ruth Fry. "Rhododendron, Our State Flower: Talk Given by Mrs. Ruth Fry Epperson at the May Breakfast, 1944, of the Women's Century Club, Seattle, Wash." Unpublished manuscript, 3359. Museum of History and Industry, Seattle.

Fahey, John. "The Nevada Bloomer Case." *Columbia* 2, no. 2 (Summer 1988): 42–45.

Fowler, Robert Booth. "Carrie Chapman Catt, Strategist." In *One Woman, One Vote*, edited by Marjorie Spruill Wheeler, 295–314. Troutdale, Ore.: NewSage Press, 1995.

Geiger, Gary L. "Adele Parker: The Case Study of a Woman in the Progressive Era." Master's thesis, Western Washington University, 1979.

Gillis, Emalee Gruss. "May Arkwright Hutton and the Battle for Women's Suffrage." *Pacific Northwest Inlander* (March 6–12, 2008): 16–21.

Haarsager, Sandra. *Bertha Knight Landes of Seattle: Big City Mayor*. Norman: University of Oklahoma Press, 1994.

———. *Organized Womanhood: Cultural Politics in the Pacific Northwest, 1840–1920*. Norman: University of Oklahoma Press, 1997.

Horner, Patricia Voeller. "May Arkwright Hutton: Suffragist and Politician." In *Women in Pacific Northwest History: An Anthology*, edited by Karen Blair. Seattle: University of Washington Press, 1988.

Hynding, Alan. *The Public Life of Eugene Semple, Promoter and Politician of the Northwest*. Seattle: University of Washington Press, 1973.

Irwin, Inez Haynes. *The Story of Alice Paul and the National Woman's Party*, 1921 (reprint). Fairfax, Va.: Denlingers Publishers, Inc., 1977.

Jennings, Linda, ed. *Washington Women's Cook Book*. Seattle: Trade Register Print, 1909.

Johnson, Claudius O. "George Turner: Part I, The Background of a Statesman." *Pacific Northwest Quarterly* 34 (1943): 243–69.

———. "George Turner: Part II, United States Senator and Counsel and Arbiter for the United States." *Pacific Northwest Quarterly* 34 (1943): 367–92.

Kerr, William T. "The Progressive of Washington, 1910–12." *Pacific Northwest Quarterly* 55 (January 1964): 16–27.

Kessler-Harris, Alice. *Out to Work*. New York: Oxford University Press, 1982.

Kizer, Benjamin H. "May Arkwright Hutton." *Pacific Northwest Quarterly* 57 (1966): 49–56.

Larson, T. Alfred. "Emancipating the West's Dolls, Vassals, and Hopeless Drudges: The Origins of Woman Suffrage in the West." In *Essays in Western History in Honor of T. A. Larson*, edited by Roger Daniels. Laramie: University of Wyoming Publications, 1971.

———. "The Woman Suffrage Movement in Washington." *Pacific Northwest Quarterly* 67, no. 2 (April 1976): 49–62.

———. "Woman's Rights in Idaho." *Idaho Yesterdays* 16 (Spring 1971): 2–15.

Lippincott, Marianne. "Women's Legislative Council of Washington November, 1917 to May 1938." Unpublished manuscript, 1980. James E. Brooks Library, Central Washington University, Ellensburg.

McDonald, Lucile. "The Battle over the State Flower." *Seattle Times Magazine* (January 31, 1965): 2.

Mead, Rebecca. *How the Vote Was Won*. New York: New York University Press, 2004.

Mires, Austin. "Remarks on the Constitution of the State of Washington." *Washington Historical Quarterly* 22, no. 4 (1931): 276–88.

Montgomery, James. *Liberated Woman*. Fairfield, Wash.: Ye Galleon Press, 1985.

Morgan, Murray. "Washington Women's Roller Coaster Ride to the Franchise." In *Pacific Northwest: Essays in Honor of James W. Scott*, edited by Howard J. Critchfield. Bellingham: Western Washington University, 1993.

Moynihan, Ruth Barnes. *Rebel for Rights*. New Haven, Conn.: Yale University Press, 1983.

Murphy, John Miller. "Woman Suffrage in Washington Territory." In *Souvenir of Western Women*, edited by Mary Osborn Douthit. Portland: Anderson Duniway, 1905.

National American Woman Suffrage Association. *Victory: How Women Won It: A Centennial Symposium*. New York: H. W Wilson Company, 1940.

National League for Woman's Service. *Washington State Report for 1917–1919*. N.p., n.d.

Newell, Gordon. *Rogues, Buffoons, and Statesmen.* Seattle: Superior Publishing Company, 1975.

Oberdeck, Kathryn J. "'Not Pink Teas': The Seattle Working-Class Women's Movement, 1905–1918." *Labor History* 32 (1991): 193–230.

Pacey, Mary Susan. "The Breakthrough State: The Washington State Suffrage Campaign of 1906–1910." Master's thesis, University of Washington, 1978.

Parry, Janine A. "Putting Feminism to a Vote: The Washington State Women's Council, 1963–1978." *Pacific Northwest Quarterly* 91, no. 4 (Fall 2000): 171–82.

Paynter, Susan. "The Fight for Equal Rights: A Fifty-Year Struggle for Change." *Seattle Post-Intelligencer,* July 30–August 11, 1972.

Pierce, Stella E. "Suffrage in the Pacific Northwest: Old Oregon and Washington." *Washington Historical Quarterly* 3 (April 1912): 106–14.

Pieroth, Doris. "Women's Suffrage: No Constitutional Franchise." *Columbia* 3, no. 2 (Summer 1989): 22–23.

———. "Bertha Knight Landes: The Woman Who Was Mayor." In *Women in Pacific Northwest History,* edited by Karen J. Blair, rev. ed., 83-106. Seattle: University of Washington Press, 2001.

Putnam, John. "A 'Test of Chiffon Politics': Gender Politics in Seattle, 1897–1917." In "Woman Suffrage: The View from the Pacific," special issue, *Pacific Historical Review* 69, no. 4 (November 2000): 595–616.

———. "The Emergence of a New West: The Politics of Class and Gender in Seattle, 1880-1917." PhD diss., University of California, San Diego, 2000.

Reese, Michael. "To Help Her Live the Right Kind of Life—Mothers' Pensions in King County, 1913–1937." In *More Voices, New Stories: King County, Washington's First 150 Years.,* edited by Mary C. Wright. Seattle: King County Landmarks & Heritage Commission, 2002.

Riley, Glenda. *Inventing the American Woman: An Inclusive History.* Vol. 2, *Since 1877.* Wheeling, Ill.: Harlan Davidson, 2001.

Rosenow, Beverly Paulik, ed. *Journal of the Washington State Constitutional Convention, 1889.* Seattle: Book Publishing Company, 1962.

Ross-Nazzal, Jennifer. "Always Be Good Natured and Cheerful': Emma Smith DeVoe and the Woman Suffrage Movement." PhD diss., Washington State University, 2004.

———. "Emma Smith DeVoe: Practicing Pragmatic Politics in the Pacific Northwest." *Pacific Northwest Quarterly* 96, no. 2 (Spring 2005): 76–84.

Rupp, Liela J. and Verta Taylor. *Survival in the Doldrums: The American Women's Rights Movement, 1945 to the 1960s.* New York: Oxford University Press, 1987.

Scharff, Virginia. *Taking the Wheel: Women and the Coming of the Motor Age.* Toronto: Collier Macmillan Canada, 1991.

Seiber, Richard A., ed. *Memoirs of Puget Sound: Early Seattle, 1853–1856. The Letters of David & Catherine Blaine.* Fairfield, Wash.: Ye Galleon Press, 1978.

Severn, Jill. *The State We're In: Washington, Your Guide to State, Tribal and Local Government.* Seattle: The League of Women Voters Education Fund, 2004.

Sheeran, Marte Jo. "The Woman Suffrage Issue in Washington, 1890–1910." Master's thesis, University of Washington, 1977.

Sherlock, Margaret V. "The Recall of Mayor Gill." *Pacific Monthly* 26, no. 2 (August 1911): 117–30.

Simmons, Clyde B. "The History of Woman Suffrage in the State of Washington." Master's thesis, University of Washington, 1903.

Soden, Dale. *The Reverend Mark Matthews: An Activist in the Progressive Era.* Seattle: University of Washington Press, 2001.

Stanton, Elizabeth Cady, Susan B. Anthony, Matilda Joslyn Gage, and Ida Husted Harper, eds. *History of Woman Suffrage,* 6 vols. Rochester: J. J. Little and Ives Co., 1881–1922.

Stevenson, Shanna. "November 1883: When Washington Women First Won the Right To Vote." *Olympian Totem Tidings,* November 20, 1983, 5.

Strasser, Susan, *Never Done: A History of American Housework.* New York: Henry Holt and Company, 1982.

Suderman, Hannelore. "History Was Made…The Fight for Equity for Women's Athletics in Washington." *Washington State Magazine* (Fall 2007). http://washington-state-magazine.wsu.edu/stories/2007/November/history.html.

Sylvia Van Kirk, *Many Tender Ties: Women in the Fur-Trade Society, 1670–1870.* Norman: University of Oklahoma, 1983.

Taber, Ronald. "Sacajawea and the Suffragettes." *Pacific Northwest Quarterly* 58, no. 1 (January 1967): 7–13.

Van Burkleo, Sandra F. "'A Double Head in Nature is a Monstrosity': Re-Covering the Married Woman in Frontier Washington, 1879–1892." Paper presented, Annual Meeting of the American Society for Legal History, Seattle, Wash., October 21–24, 1998.

"Washington's First Constitution, 1878." *Washington Historical Quarterly* 9 (1918): 139–40.

Washington Secretary of State, Division of Archives. "Women's Rights in Washington State: An Issue of the 80's, Historical Documents, 1884–1915." From *Journeys to the Past,* a collection of facsimile documents for Washington State history, n.d., Olympia.

Washington Territorial Legislature. *Speech of Hon. D. R. Bigelow on Female Suffrage Delivered in the House of Representatives of Washington Territorial Legislature, October, 14, 1871.* Olympia: Washington Territorial Legislature, 1871.

Wellman, Judith. *The Road to Seneca Falls: Elizabeth Cady Stanton and the First Woman's Rights Convention.* Urbana: University of Illinois Press, 2004.

Withers, Jean, Lynn Morrison, Ruth Jones, and Fredericka Foster. *The Women of Ellensburg: Report of the Washington State International Women's Year Conference,* 1977, n.p., 1977.

Woloch, Nancy. *Women and the American Experience.* Vol. 2, *From 1860.* New York: McGraw-Hill, 1994.

Credits

Alice Paul Institute, Inc.: 62

Bryn Mawr College Library, Carrie Chapman Catt Collection: 30 (right)

Lynn Chao: 73

Clallam County Museum: 31, 33

Confederated Tribes of the Colville Reservation, family of Lucy Covington: 87 (upper)

Corbis: 78

Corbis, Bettman Archive: ii, xii, 2, 70 (upper)

Kathryn Crossley: 24 (lower)

Elizabeth Haines: 52 (right)

David Hansen: 79, 86 (lower)

The Huntington Library: 69

Library of Congress: 10 (lower), 18, 38, 48, 49 (lower), 57 (lower), 71

The Museum of Flight: x

Museum of History and Industry: viii, 7, 32, 54 (top right), 56 (left)

National Aeronautics and Space Administration: 89

National Women's Rights Historic Park: 4

Nebraska State Historical Society: 9

Northwest Museum of Arts and Culture/Eastern Washington State Historical Society: vi–vii, 25 (upper), 42, 56 (right)

Office of Senator Maria Cantwell: 83 (center left)

Office of the Clerk, U.S. House of Representatives: 88 (upper)

Office of the Governor of Washington State: 83 (center right)

Oregon Historical Society: 11, 16, 39 (upper)

Radcliffe Library: 37

The Saeger Family: 8 (right)

Schlesinger Library, Radcliffe House, Harvard University: 59 (upper)

Seattle Municipal Archives: 45

The Seattle Times, Richard Heyza photo: 87 (lower)

Sewall-Belmont House and Museum: 70 (lower), 72, 98, 102

Sisters of Providence Archives: 84

Shanna Stevenson, Boston Harbor Photography photo: back cover flap

Tacoma Public Library: 43

Dora Tréviño: 88 (lower)

University of Washington Libraries, Special Collections Division: 14, 26, 74–75, 86 (upper)

Washington Park Alliance, Greg Vaughn photo: 36

Washington State Archives: 12, 25 (lower), 41, 49 (upper), 55 (lower), 66, 76, 82 (right and center)

Washington State Historical Society, Museum and Special Collections: inside cover, back cover, i, v, 3, 6, 8 (left), 10 (upper), 13, 15, 17, 19, 20, 22, 24 (upper), 27, 28, 30 (left), 34, 35 (upper right), 39 (lower), 40, 44, 47 (right), 50, 51, 53, 54 (left), 55 (upper), 58, 61, 63, 64, 65, 67, 68, 74 (lower), 77, 80, 82 (buttons), 83 (right), 94, 95, 96, 100, 105

Washington State Library: 52 (left)

Washington State Library, Emma Smith DeVoe Collection: 47 (left), 57 (upper), 59 (lower)

Washington State Senate: 83 (left)

Washington State University and Pictopia.com (photo credit to Rod Commons): 81

Washington State University, Special Collections: 91

Whatcom Museum of History and Art : 46

Whitman College and Northwest Archives: 29

The Woman's Century Club of Seattle: 21, 23, 35

Index

A–C

Abortion, 81
Adams, Abigail, 3
ADC. *See* Aid to Dependent Children
AERA. *See* American Equal Rights Association
African Americans, 22, 73, 86
Aid to Families with Dependent Children, 66
Alaska–Yukon–Pacific Exposition, 47, 50, 58
Alcohol, 68
Alki Suffrage Club, 21, 49, 55
Allyn, Frank, 28
Amendments, 5, 8, 44–45, 72–73, 77–81. *See also specific Amendment*
American Association of University Women, 22
American Equal Rights Association, 5
American Indian Women's Service League, 22
"American Woman and Her Peers," 58
American Woman Suffrage Association, 5, 71
Anthony, Susan B., 5, 8–11, 37
Anti-discrimination legislation, 80
Anti-liquor legislation, 25–26
Anti-suffrage efforts, 35
Anti-suffrage law, 11
Apple Orchard Convention, 24
Asberry, Nettie J., 22, 86
Athletics, 81
Automobiles, 40
AWSA. *See* American Woman Suffrage Association
Axtell, Frances C., 82
Bagley, Clarence, 18, 24, 29
Baker, Elizabeth, 51
Baker, LaReine, 48, 51, 58
Ballots, 30–31
Bell, T. J., 45
Bicycle, 40
Bigelow, Ann Elizabeth White, 9–10
Bigelow, Daniel, 9–10
Black River, 8
Blackwell, Alice, 50
Blackwell, Antoinette Brown, 38–39
Blackwell, Henry, 5, 29, 37–38, 56

Blaine, Catharine Paine, 7
Blaine, David, 7
Blair, Karen, 20, 22, 32
Blair v. Washington State University, 81
Blatch, Harriet Stanton, 70
Bloomer, Nevada, 27–28
"Blue Liner," 40
Bradshaw, Charles M., 24
Brady, James H., 56, 69
Briggs-Wall, Henrietta, 58
Brooks, Benton, 56
Brown, Alfred, 59
Brown, Beria, 10
Brown, Leonia, 48
Brown, Mary Olney, 8, 14, 20
Burke, Thomas, 27
Van Burkleo, Sandra, 31
Burns, Lucy, 69–70, 72
Business and Professional Women, 22
Camp Equality, 52
Campaigns, 53–55, 59–60
Campbell, John, 67
Campfire Girls, 22
Cantwell, Maria, 83
Carlyon, Philip H., 73
Case, Charles R., 52
Catt, Carrie Chapman, 21, 23, 35, 44, 55, 71
Cayton, Susie Revels, 22
Chautauquas, 57
Chicago Columbian Exposition, 33
Chinese Exclusion Act, 27–28
Chinese immigrants, 27–28, 73
Chong Wa Benevolent Association, 22
Chow, Ruby, 87
Churches, 51
Chused, Richard H., 12
Citizenship, 73
Civil Rights Act (1964), 81
Civil War, 20–21
Clubs, 20–23, 34–35, 41–42, 49, 65
Coates, Sadie, 52
Colby, Clara Bewick, 29–30, 56
College education, 41
College Equal Suffrage League, The, 41, 49

Colorado, 61
Colorado Equal Suffrage Association, 57
Colored Ladies' Society, 22
Colors, 71
Columbia Maternal Association, 23
Comegys, George, 14
Community property laws, 12, 15
Comparable worth, 82
Congressional Union, 69–70
Constitutional Convention, 29–30
Consumer's League, 23
Cott, Nancy F., 64
Cotterill, George, 44–45
Council of Women Voters, 65
Covington, Lucy Friedlander, 87
Cowlitz River, 9
Crannell, W. Winslow, 35
Croake, Nena J., 82
Cummings, Fanny Leake, 39, 41
Cyclop, 10

D–F

Daily Oregonian, 18
Davies, Margery W., 40
de Mattos, James P., 34
Declaration of Sentiments, 4, 6–7
Demonstrations, 70
Denny, Arthur A., 6–7, 51
Denny, Emily Inez, 51
Denny, Mary Ann Boren, 7
DeVoe, Emma Smith, 21, 41, 43, 45, 48, 51, 67, 69, 73
Dimmick, Carolyn, 83
Discrimination, 80
Dix, Augusta, 21
Doane, William Croswell, 51
Dorcas Charity Club, 22
Dubois, Ellen Carol, 8, 75
Dunbar, Bonnie, 89
Duniway, Abigail Scott
  campaigning by, 56
  celebration on passage of suffrage bill, 19–20
  description of, 9, 38
  illustration of, 11, 16